"Relationships are always in motion, always moving, always becoming. *Friendlationships* explores the murky waters where love and friendship are the hardest to navigate, but also the place where we discover new parts of ourselves, others, and God."
—*STEPHEN JAMES*, psychotherapist and author,
Becoming a Dad: A Spiritual, Emotional and Practical Guide

"I never thought it would be possible for anyone to rationally explain the different yet interconnected topics of Christian friendships and relationships; that is, of course, until I read *Friendlationships*. Through witty narration, relevant examples, and God-centered insight, Jeff's book sheds an authentically helpful light on the somewhat controversial topic of dating within the Christian community."
—*LINDSEY KANE*, independent singer/songwriter

"Thank goodness someone finally said out loud the word we've all been thinking (and living) for so long—friendlationships—that weird, in-between scenario that mystifies and terrifies. If you've ever had a friend say, 'What's going on with you two, are you dating or what?' and your response was, 'Uhhhh, I don't know ...'—read this book."
—*JOANNA HARRIS*, author, *You Didn't Complete Me: When the One Turns Out to Be Just Someone*

"Jeff talks from this generation to this generation. *Friendlationships* is an entertaining, candid look at things that need to be talked about that no one else is talking about. In conversational style, Jeff uses lots of personal experiences and stories to communicate practical advice to the one striving to navigate the often-treacherous road from like, to *like* like, to love. I heartily recommend *Friendlationships*."
—*JOHN STRAPPAZON*, collegiate ministries specialist, Baptist General Convention of Oklahoma

"Jeff's approach to this topic will speak deeply to young singles. Steering clear of formulas and quick-fix ideas, he challenges his readers to be mature and honest about themselves, their expectations, and their feelings. What a concept. Where others might prescribe methodology, Jeff Taylor shares stories and calls young singles to act like responsible adults."
—*JUSTIN McROBERTS*, independent singer/songwriter

From Like, to *Like Like*, to Love in Your Twenties

FRIENDLATIONSHIPS

Jeff Taylor

[RELEVANTBOOKS]

Published by Relevant Books
A division of Relevant Media Group, Inc.

www.relevantbooks.com
www.relevantmediagroup.com

© 2005 Relevant Media Group

Design by Relevant Solutions
Cover design by Mark Arnold
Interior design by Jeremy Kennedy

Relevant Books is a registered trademark of Relevant Media Group, Inc., and is
registered in the U.S. Patent and Trademark Office.

ALL RIGHTS RESERVED
No part of this publication may be reproduced, stored in a retrieval system,
or transmitted, in any form or by any means—electronic, mechanical,
photocopying, recording, or otherwise—without prior written permission.

All Scripture quotations are taken from the HOLY Bible, NEW
INTERNATIONAL VERSION®. NIV®. Copyright©1973, 1978, 1984 by
International Bible Society. Used by permission of Zondervan Publishing
House. All rights reserved.

Library of Congress Control Number: 2005902182
International Standard Book Number: 0-9763642-1-2

For information or bulk orders:
RELEVANT MEDIA GROUP, INC.
100 SOUTH LAKE DESTINY DR. STE. 200
ORLANDO, FL 32810
407-660-1411

05 06 07 08 9 8 7 6 5 4 3 2 1

Printed in the United States of America

THIS BOOK IS DEDICATED TO MY WIFE, ALISON.
THANKS FOR ALL OF YOUR SUPPORT AND LOVE.

CONTENTS

FOREWORD

This is just a shot in the dark, but I'm guessing that you probably picked up this book for one of two reasons. The first reason could be that you wanted further explanation on the word *friendlationship* because it seemed like such a foreign term. The other reason would be that you immediately knew what a friendlationship was (regardless of whether or not you've ever heard the word) because you've been in at least one friendlationship before, and you're probably in one now.

For those of you who fall under the first category, fear not—Jeff Taylor explains the word in full detail, so you won't be left wondering for long! For those of you in the second category, buckle up, because the conclusions you've previously reached about male-female friendships and relationships may be entirely different when you finish reading this book!

I'm not afraid to admit that I speak from an embarrassing amount of experience on this particular topic. Like many of the people you'll read about in this book, I have been in my fair share of friendlationships. I've had my heart broken, hardened, numbed, and restored. It was a wild ride ... exhilarating and uncertain, familiar and foreign all at once ... and I'm not sure if it was worth all that it cost me.

I am so grateful that Jeff has written this book, because I believe that single people in the Christian community are especially subject to the potential friendlationship. Many of us have "kissed dating goodbye," but we've unwittingly replaced those dating relationships with friendships. We seek to fill that void (either consciously or subconsciously), and we do it in a couple of different ways—either through relationships with a "stand-in girlfriend" or "stand-in boyfriend" or through having a large number of friends of the opposite sex. It's just a question of "quality versus quantity."

Let's face it—dating has become less popular these days. "Hanging out" and "hooking up" are the favored alternatives. I've heard both sexes complain that they will often "hang out" with a friend of the opposite sex, and they don't even know if they're on a date because things are left so open-ended. Chances are, you've probably had one of these thoughts: *"Is he interested in me? I can't tell."* or *"Am I supposed to pay for her movie? Does she think this is a date or not?"* In a world where blurred lines and ambiguity are easier than definition and commitment, friendlationships have a fertile breeding ground. But it all seems so harmless and casual, right?

What woman hasn't wanted to be Sally (Meg Ryan) from *When Harry Met Sally* (the definitive "friendlationship" movie)? And what guy wouldn't want to be Chandler (Matthew Perry) from *Friends* who gets to date and marry Monica (Courtney Cox-Arquette)? It seems ideal to fall in love with your best friend, doesn't it? And sometimes that happens. But sometimes the reality is more like *Seinfeld*. If you remember, Jerry (Jerry Seinfeld) and Elaine (Julia Louis-Dreyfus) didn't end up together.

So what do we do? Do we avoid friendships with the opposite sex? Do we press on in these friendships anyway? Do we only become friends with people we would date? So many questions!

Thankfully, Jeff has managed to handle the topic with humor, grace, and honesty. He uses some of my favorite examples from movies, books, songs, and television shows to help drive the point home. These are things that you and I can relate to directly, because they've been such a strong force in our culture. And let's be honest, sometimes it's just easier to see the truth when it's someone else's story that you're examining, instead of your own.

Navigating male-female friendships and potential relationships is certainly not easy, but this book serves as a great "field guide." I've been challenged by Jeff's words, and I believe that you will be, too.

Tara Leigh Cobble
Independent musician
www.taraleighcobble.com

ACKNOWLEDGMENTS

I would be remiss in not thanking the following people for all of their support and encouragement:

Alison, Clark, Mom, Dad, Steve, Jana, Rick, Cathy, Spencer, Mamaw, Papaw, Grandpa, Granny (RIP), Isaac, Brenda, Brittany, Chris, Terry, David, Sarah, Randall, Cathy, Jennifer, Michael, Austin, Janice, Lavinia, the Hitts, the Motsenbockers, the Polittes, the Craigs, the Corks, the Sosebees, John and Wanda Strappazon, Jon Randles, Scott and Sharlain Donaho, Tyson and Melissa Williams, Hoover, C-Wag, the Lents, the Coopers, Dee, Regan, Heather, Megan, Molly, Kim, Becky,

Dane, Shari, Merrill, Matt, Cauble, Dave, the Cofields, Julia, the Jacksons, Michael, the Morgans, the Millers, the Allens, Toni, Kelsey, Emily, Bill and Diane Davis, the Trooks, the Andersons, the Arterburns, Stoughton, Tyler, the Todds, Beck, the Carters, Pearce, Ryan, the Langfords, the Johnsons, Darek, and everyone else at 9:30 Ministries and Paradigm, Cara, Jeff, Summer, Tyler, and everyone else at Relevant for giving me this once-in-a-lifetime opportunity.

Finally, I would like to thank my Lord and Savior Jesus Christ for giving me more than I ever thought possible. All glory to Him!

CHAPTER ONE

WHY KISS DATING GOODBYE?

Meet Graham. Graham is your typical Christian guy: polite, friendly, and funny. He plays the guitar and writes music and goes to college. Graham is a popular guy who, for one reason or another, does not go out on very many dates. Well, one day he asks Brittany out, and she says "yes." He is very excited, but at the same time nervous because this is his first date since high school.

Graham goes to Brittany's house to pick her up, and they are hanging out in her room talking before they leave. As they chat, Graham's stomach slowly starts knotting up inside

1

of him. Soon enough, he cannot even focus on what she is saying; he is so concerned with calming down.

Finally, he mutters, "Can I use your restroom?"

She tells him that he can, and he goes to calm himself down. To give you a picture of the situation, he is staring in her mirror saying, "Be cool, man; this is ridiculous; don't be doing this." Finally he leaves the bathroom and, as he walks out the door, realizes that he did not even flush the toilet or turn on the faucet to cover for his nervousness. He sits back down, and they continue talking. Once again, the butterflies in his stomach become overwhelming, and he excuses himself to the bathroom for personal pep rally number two.

Once again, he forgets to flush or turn on the faucet. At this point, he finally confesses, "Sorry, I am just really nervous about this date."

> "There are three things that are too amazing for me, four that I do not understand: the way of an eagle in the sky, the way of a snake on a rock, the way of a ship on the high seas, and the way of a man with a maiden."
>
> —*PROVERBS 30:18-19*

Brittany suggests that they go ahead and leave so that he might calm down. As they get to the driveway, he starts feeling anxious again. As she is talking with him, the world starts spinning faster and faster. Acting on instinct, Graham takes two steps to the side and vomits all over Brittany's driveway. He looks up to see shock and concern on her face. He vomits again. He looks up, and she is gone.

Graham does not have time to worry about her departure because he is busy trying to exorcise that day's lunch from his digestive system. Brittany comes running back to him, although she is not alone; she went to get help. From a neighbor? Oh no, that would have been embarrassing. No, no. Brittany went to get her mom.

So, on Graham's first date with Brittany, he vomits and helps her mom clean their driveway. And do you know where Graham and Brittany are today?

Well, they never went out again.

What did you think I was going to say?

The history of dating is not one of successes (though they exist) but one of many, many failures. Why is that? What about dealing with the opposite sex makes us so awkward and weird? Why would Jake throw a surprise birthday party for his girlfriend that consisted of stuffed animals in party hats? Why is it even weirder in the context of the Church?

Are we designed to be this awkward in our dating experiences? I think not, but the reality of our awkwardness speaks for itself. I think this explains why there are so many books on dating and relationships on the market; there is something wrong, and we are trying to fix it. There are problems affecting Christians, specifically those in early adulthood, which are not being addressed.

So, I stopped by my nearest Barnes & Noble bookstore the other day, just to be sure.

Wedged in the Relationship section with dozens and dozens of sex books were some of the following tomes dedicated to healthy relationships:

Make Every Girl Want You

Ladies, did you know that you are powerless against the information in this book? Any guy who reads this will be irresistible. Of course, you need to realize that this book is not about relationships; it is about getting someone in bed. That is not acting in love; it is merely trying to satisfy one's own desires at the expense of others.

Mr. Right, Right Now!: How a Smart Woman Can Land Her Dream Man in 6 Weeks

If you are a dumb woman, it takes you a little bit longer. But seriously, who needs prayer? With this book, your ideal guy is just six weeks away. Forget seeking God and just read this book!

How Can You Tell if You're Really in Love?

Three words: You. Just. Know. Really, if you have to use a checklist or a book to tell you that you are in love, then there might be a problem. "Oh sorry, Doug; you scored a six out of ten on the quiz. I guess I really do not love you."

Are You Normal?

Too many jokes, too many jokes. This book is great because it really puts the focus where it needs to be in a relationship: on a person's shortcomings and insecurities.

How to Attract Anyone, Anytime, Anyplace

Hint: It takes magnets. Lots and lots of magnets. But in all honesty I know that this book works. How do you think Pedro got his sweet skills at hooking up with girls? It was not the fact that his bike could go off those sweet jumps (although it never hurts to get three feet of air).

How to Get Your Lover Back

In other words, read this book and learn how to lose your self-esteem and solidify the fact that you are not an individual, but someone who is defined by those around you.

Do you notice any themes? There seems to be a lot of focus on individuals, on attracting anyone, on finding Mr. Right in six weeks. Attracting anyone? Is that love, or is that wanting to be loved and needed by others? People are desperate for love and attention, but if they do not seek love in its proper perspective, they will end up lonely and craving something that no one can give them. These books are teaching the wrong perspectives on relationships and are leading people down a path of pain and mistrust. Relationships are about sacrifice and giving, not about how the other person makes you feel. Books like these deny Christ's love; therefore, they have no clue how to deal with true love.

> "Fell in love at 22 with a girl that's close to you."
> — "FELL IN LOVE AT 22," STARFLYER 59

Fair enough; I will just stop by my local Christian bookstore and see what type of help is being offered by my brothers and sisters in Christ. I found several books promoting courtship. The problem that I have heard from a significant number of people is the blurry line between friendship and courtship. "Where does one end and the other begin? Why do they act like my friend one day and my SigOth (commonly known as Significant Other) the next?"

In the Christian subculture, it seems as if there are two target audiences when it comes to relationship books: married/engaged couples and teenagers. I cannot help but wonder where the books designed for the single young adult are.

The Christian subculture is a unique one. There are relationship issues that believers go through that no one else does. What do you do when you become attracted to someone who is married? How do I forgive myself for going too far? How does one go from being friends to something more? What does spiritual leadership mean in the age of feminism? There are countless other questions that I hope to address here.

"For this reason a man will leave his father and mother and be united to his wife, and the two will become one flesh. This is a profound mystery."

—*EPHESIANS 5:31-32*

I will also address, through The Real Man Survey and The Actual Female Survey, just what Christian men and women are looking for in a romantic partner. Fifty men and fifty women each filled out a survey regarding relationships, and the results were fascinating. The results will be discussed in the context of the chapters, but the full results are contained as appendices at the end of the book.

Traditionally, the Church has offered two schools of thought on dating: "it did not exist in biblical times and therefore should not be practiced now" and "everything in dating is acceptable as long as you do not have sex."

I would like to look at each of these thoughts in turn.

Philosophy #1: Dating did not exist in biblical times and therefore should not be practiced now.

This is an outdated mode of thought and, as any effective youth minister or young adult leader can attest, is an exercise in futility to teach. Society today equates love and relationships with dating; we have been programmed to have a desire to love and be loved. People today express love and interest through dating and asking others out. To ignore this situation because it is "not the way you were raised" is to allow the devil a foothold in a place where churches can least afford it.

I will state that another way: Our churches are slowly dying because of the horrible relationship decisions that their members make. That, along with the fact that many church leaders refuse to face reality and deal with twenty-first-century problems leads to people being disenfranchised with the Church and its own members feeling like they are drowning in the deep end of the pool. This must be stopped. My friends, the problem will not go away if we ignore it. This problem has festered long enough because the Church, on the whole, has been negligent in addressing these uncomfortable issues.

Philosophy #2: Everything in dating is acceptable as long as you do not have sex.

Premarital sex is one of the banes of the Church's existence. True Love Waits programs and promise rings permeate youth activities throughout the year. Do not get me wrong; these programs are awesome, and young people and adults should likewise be taught that sex is to be saved for marriage. However, other forms of intimacy that are not discussed are killing relationships and forcing people to leave with bitterness and discontent. Emotional and spiritual intimacy should be saved for married couples, yet we throw them away every time we date someone in the hope that they will love us. The sad part is that church leaders are doing nothing to stop it; either they do not feel it is necessary, or they simply do not know how to put an end to it.

This book is not a quick help guide. No worthwhile book is. If you want to become stronger in your relationships, then it will take a lot of time and effort. I am here to help you start on that long road. I will offer various tips and suggestions, but do not think that they are the only road to success.

The stories shared within are true. Some of these stories might sound familiar, probably because they have happened to you as well.

So, now that you know what to expect, kick back in your chair, turn on a rerun of *Friends*, and let's spend some time looking at the time that is our twenties.

Oh yeah, and make sure you flush the toilet next time.

CHAPTER TWO

A DATE, DATING, AND THE DTR

Meet Emily. Emily gets accepted to Texas A&M University. The summer prior to her freshman year, she's invited to a barbecue for incoming freshmen from her hometown. She goes, hoping to meet some people and develop some connections. She meets a guy at the barbecue named Joe. Joe is very nice, well mannered, with a great personality. However, he's not really her type. He is not very attractive, and she just does not feel a connection. After some conversation, he asks her for her digits. Since she is a shy eighteen-year-old who does not know what else to do, she gives him her number, hoping he will not call.

That works about as well as you could guess.

A couple of days later, he calls her and asks if she wants to go to a movie. Emily has a problem saying "no thanks," so she agrees to go, with one condition: she has to meet him at the theater. When Joe asks her why she feels the need to do that, Emily replies that she does it on all her first dates as a safety factor (blatant lie). Poor Joe agrees to meet her there that Friday night. At the theater, they strike up a conversation before the movie starts, which leads to more awkwardness; every pet peeve that Emily despises Joe uses unknowingly with reckless abandon. Then the movie starts, and it doesn't get much better. The movie is horrible, but Emily makes it through without touching Joe, trying to send hints that she is not really interested. Finally the movie ends, and he walks her to her car. When they get to the car, he asks her if she would like to go out again sometime. At this point Emily has had her fill of awkwardness and is ready to burst. She clearly does not want to go out again, but instead of just saying "no thanks," she tries to break it to him in a different language, the original language of love: Latin. Pig Latin, to be precise. He asks her out and she replies, "Ix-nay on the ating-day." Needless to say, they never went out again. I mean, once you get turned down in Pig Latin, there is not really any point, is there?

> "My words don't come out easily. So I will tell you honestly. No one wants to spend eternity alone."
>
> —"THE FINAL SLOW DANCE," MXPX

The asking-out aspect of dating is perhaps the most stressful and confusing one. It takes a big risk and promises little in return. With any interpersonal dynamic, communication is key. Our words are a threshold that catalogs our relationship as it progresses deeper and deeper. At first, a smile from someone is all it takes for you to feel as if you are on top of the world, and then the smile is replaced by kind words, etc. Each stage is significant and indicative of the state of the relationship, and each stage begins with the crossing of the communication border. To be more specific, the threshold that guys and girls cross to deepen their relationship—or to cut it off—is known as the Define the Relationship talk (hereby known as "DTR"). The DTR is a conversation designed to clarify the nature of two individuals' association, for the relationship to either progress or end.

There are multiple uses for the DTR. The most common use of the DTR is the aforementioned asking out. One person sees potential in a dating relationship and begins a dialogue to see if the other person sees it as well. Perhaps the most stressful aspect of the asking-out part is defining the event as a date or not.

WHAT IS A DATE?

I asked the individuals who took each survey to define, in their own words, the word *date*. The results were very interesting. I have chosen to divide the responses between guys and girls to see if there are any gender discrepancies (full results are in the appendices).

Here are some of the responses from the ladies:

"A date involves a guy asking a girl if he can hang out with her with the intention of getting to know her in a way that is deeper than just a friendship. A date can involve a meal, a movie, a game, etc. There is no defined 'date,' just the date itself."

"A 'date,' I think, would be the traditional situation in which a guy and a girl go out alone or in a group—but does not necessarily imply 'romance' or the possibility of a future relationship."

"A date is an emotionally casual outing for the purpose of getting to know a member of the opposite sex better. Dating more than one person at a time is acceptable."

"It is just the two of you, and no one has defined it as a 'just friends' outing. (Note, if there hasn't been any sort of definition, most girls would consider alone-time with a guy a date.)"

Notice any themes? Notice any disparities? One girl said that the date is with the intention of going deeper, and another said that there does not have to be the possibility of a dating relationship. One person said that having dates with more than one person is acceptable while another thinks the date implies exclusive interest.

Interesting. Let's see what the guys had to say before I comment any further:

"Date: previously agreed upon get-together between two people (of the opposite sex) with the UNDERSTOOD intention to set the stage for a possible romantic relationship."

"If a guy asks a girl out as more than a friend but the girl doesn't feel the same, then no matter what the guy says to me, that's not a date."

So, these guys say that there has to be an understanding on both sides that there is, in fact, potential in a relationship for it to be considered a date. It is safe to say that people have varying definitions of *date* and that most of the awkwardness in relationships might come from differing or conflicting views on what constitutes a date. For the remainder of this book, I will be basing my idea of *date* on this definition:

"Two individuals spending time together with the possibility of romance."

I feel there is enough room for interpretation with it to satisfy everyone. If there is no possibility of romance, then it is simply hanging out with someone of the opposite sex. For the initial dates, asking the other person plays an integral role.

HOW TO TELL IF SOMEONE WANTS TO GO OUT WITH YOU

There is so much focus on what constitutes a date that we often forget about the intricacies that go into asking someone out. You cannot have a date (in the sense that I define it) without asking someone out. The first step that must be established is to see whether or not the person being asked out on a date will say "yes."

For most individuals, if they have feelings for someone else (or are just attracted to them), they will do one of many things:

She will wuss out and never talk to him again or be really awkward when she does.

This is also commonly known as playing "hard to get." "Hard to get" is one of the most confusing ways to show that you like someone. It sends the exact opposite message and often prevents the relationship that you so strongly desire. This is not junior high; there should not be a problem with showing your attraction to a person. But many people still choose to show their feelings this way.

She will spend all of her time around him, trying to impress him, and come off as overbearing.

This is where the words *weirdo* (for the guys) and *stalker* (for the girls) comes into play. This is the person whose friends make fun of him when they are hanging out with you, often openly mocking his methods of trying to impress you.

He looks at her when she's looking away and then quickly looks in another direction when she happens to look at him.

You should know that you are reading a book by the master of this maneuver. I developed the art of the stare/look away in history lecture. Instead of learning about the XYZ Affair, I was busy working on my neck reflexes. I was like Wally West (The Flash, for those of you who do not speak nerd). One day I got whiplash from moving so fast. This person often gets diagnosed with ADHD because the people around him think he has trouble focusing on any one object.

When walking by, he will attempt eye contact and deliver a smile (hoping that she returns both).

I had to be gender specific on this one. It is safe to say that any guy who does the eye contact/smile to a stranger thinks she is attractive. Sometimes if a girl does it, she is simply being polite. Ladies, have you ever passed a guy and smiled at him? You may have just been acting nice. Later that day he brags to his friends, "This chick was totally checking me out today at the mall."

He will try to at least be in the same social group with her at night and on the weekends just so that they can spend time together.

Observe his social patterns—does he start hanging out with your specific group more than he once did?

She will become his friend and every once in a while casually ask what his plans are for the weekend.

You see, she is nonchalantly testing the waters to see if he is dating anybody and if he might want to spend more time together.

How can a girl let a guy know that she likes him? It is a double-edged sword. Every guy's opinion is that she needs to tell him about her feelings. Whether they really want it to happen or not is open for interpretation.

If you two are already friends, there's a risk involved of things being awkward after that talk. Are you willing to risk that? These strong feelings are not going to go away. You will just kick yourself every time he goes out with someone else (more on that in the next chapter).

EXCUSES, EXCUSES

The danger of initiating a DTR is that it's your biggest chance for failure. A wise man once told me that when a guy asks a girl out, he is giving her a loaded gun and giving her permission to pull the trigger if need be.

Meet Cassie. As she is starting her freshman year of college, she hears through the grapevine that this older guy at her church likes her. She also hears that he is going to ask her out sometime soon. Each Wednesday night at college night at church she anxiously waits, but he never does. One night she thinks for sure he is going to, but he ends up leaving early. When she leaves the church, she sees him driving in circles around the building. Then as she drives away, she sees him leave the parking lot, too. He seems to be going the same direction she is, but then he makes a random turn somewhere, but again somehow meets back up with her—right behind her car. When she pulls up to her house, he pulls in behind her. She gets out, and he looks pale. She asks him if everything is alright, and he says "yes." But he doesn't say anything else. He just stands there in her driveway staring at her quietly. He then asks if she wants to get ice cream, and then he says, "Well, I mean do you want to go out with me?" And she says, "For ice cream?" He says, "No, I don't really like ice cream. I just wanted to know if you'd go out with me, and ice cream sounded like a good icebreaker in my head."

Like this guy, ladies and gentlemen both have some considerable fear that they deal with, the fear of failure and rejection. So, if a guy who you do not happen to like asks you out, please *do not put off telling him how you feel*. In the surveys, the question was posed to the ladies, "A nice guy asks you out, but you do not feel attracted to him. What would you do?" Only 34 percent would give a definitive answer ("yes" or "no, never"). The other 68 percent said "no, not at this time" or "maybe sometime in the future." Ladies, if you deliver a half-hearted, "Oh not *this* weekend, but maybe some other time" answer, *he will ask you again*. It is not fair to hold a guy's feelings captive because you are too afraid to tell him the truth. Do not be mean about it; be assertive and communicate your feelings clearly so that there will be no question about where you two stand. And guys, if a lady is giving you clear signals, respect her decision and move on.

Along those lines, I am sick and tired of seeing Christian men and women use God as an excuse in their dating life. What I mean is when you break up with someone or turn somebody down for a date with the justification of "God is calling me to be single." That is awesome if that is the case, but it is often used as a cop-out. I have seen several girls merely use this as an excuse in order to not hurt a guy's feelings. I have seen girls say to one guy that God is not calling her to date anybody, and then next week she is on a date with another guy. There are some legit, cool girls who really are not willing to date until they are "ready," and that is awesome, but there are a lot of girls who will use that as an excuse and nothing more. If a guy asks you out, just let him know how you feel. If you do not want to date him, let him know that. Sure, it will make things awkward between you, but it's like pulling off a Band-Aid: do it quickly and the pain will subside.

> "You get their phone number and you call them up and you say, 'Yeah, that's a really great phone conversation, can I see you some time?' and then they say, 'I'd like that.' Nothing feels better than 'I'd like that.'"
>
> —"ANY GIVEN THURSDAY," JOHN MAYER

But what happens when she says "yes"? What happens when she does not turn you down for a second date by speaking in Pig Latin? There is a fine line that is crossed from dating somebody to DATING somebody.

As previously stated, a date is two individuals spending time together with the possibility of romance. I feel that a dating relationship is defined as a *committed premarital relationship in which two individuals have chosen to determine whether they are compatible for marriage*. Witness this scene from *Seinfeld*. George Costanza is attempting to justify asking another woman out when he has been going on dates with Susan already.

George: "I'm not married. I'm not allowed to go out with somebody else?"

Jerry: "It depends."

George: "Depends on what?"

Jerry: "On many factors."

George: "Like what?"

Jerry: "Well, how long you've been seeing her. What's your phone call frequency? Are you on a daily?"

George: "No. Semi-daily. Four or five times a week."

Jerry: "What about Saturday nights? Do you have to ask her out, or is a date implied?"

George: "Implied."

Jerry: "She got anything in your medicine cabinet?"

George: "There might be some moisturizer."

Jerry: "Let me ask you this; is there any Tampax in your house?"

George: "Yeah."

Jerry: "Well, I'll tell you what you got here. You've got yourself a girlfriend."

The dating relationship for George has been established. Due to being in a situation where he has an implied date and consistent contact, George is officially dating Susan. Commitment has been established, and George has a girlfriend. At this point, it is appropriate for him to evaluate his chances at marriage. In fact, he and Susan would get engaged several years later and would have gotten married had it not been for poisoned envelopes.

But at this point, George did not realize that the healthy goal of a dating relationship is to see if marriage is a possibility. It is not yet another responsibility that a person should try to avoid. Why is commitment scary anyway? Is it the fear of growing up? The fear of losing these idealized childhood freedoms? The fact that another person is actually counting on you? Get over the fact that you can be a teenager for the rest of your life. God calls each of us to grow up and become men and women. The decisions that we make now will influence who we become in our thirties, forties, and beyond.

"My lover spoke and said to me, 'Arise, my darling, my beautiful one, and come with me. See! The winter is past; the rains are over and gone. Flowers appear on the earth; the season of singing has come, the cooing of doves is heard in our land. The fig tree forms its early fruit; the blossoming vines spread their fragrance. Arise, come, my darling; my beautiful one, come with me.'"

—SONG OF SOLOMON 2:10-13

21

Thus far, I have covered the positive aspects of the DTR, the DTR where the initiator desires to see the relationship deepen and progress. But there are types of DTRs when the person initiating the conversation wants things to slow down or end. This is where breakups and "Can't we just be friends" conversations occur. One of the conversations will be saved for the next chapter, the "I only like you as a friend" talk. The final DTR I would like to address is the breakup or refusal of a second date.

A question posed in the surveys was what the respondents would do if they were dating someone and realized they did not want to marry them: 52 percent of the ladies said they would break up right away (versus 36 percent of the guys), and 46 percent of the guys felt they would wait for the right time to end it (compared to 44 percent of the ladies). Do you know the truly frightening part of this question? Two ladies and five guys would either do nothing or give themselves time to come around. This belies a greater problem, the fear and disdain of being single and uncertain of a relationship future (see chapter 4).

The DTR is merely one form of communication—it is not the whole of it. Do not only use your words as a means to further a relationship or to end it; use your words in a relationship to express your feelings and to get to know the other person. If you are only talking to someone with the intention of asking them out (and not getting to know them as a person), the communication has become a means to an end and not the end itself. Loosen up, let go, and listen to what others have to say.

Oh yeah, and keep your guard up when she offers to meet you at the theater.

CHAPTER THREE

FRIENDLATIONSHIP
FAQs

Meet ... well, me. As a freshman at Texas Tech, I found myself immersed in the 9:30 college ministry scene. I had made so many friends in a short amount of time. When I first met Hannah, I did not think much else about it; after all, she was dating another guy and was older than me. No big deal, right? Well, not yet.

They broke up around the end of that first semester. Thinking nothing of it, I went on about the business of my daily routine. Around Valentine's Day, we—as a group of friends—decided to go to a special Valentine's dance that a campus ministry was sponsoring. During the dance, Hannah and I ended up dancing together, and I started getting this weird feeling that I liked her and the even weirder feeling that she liked me. You see, no girls had ever really had feelings for me before, and if they had, they did a wonderful job of hiding it. This was an altogether new experience for me.

Hannah and I started hanging out all of the time, sometimes exclusively from the rest of the group. I would see her every day, and we would just hang out and talk. It was wonderful. We started getting closer and closer, and I just knew that I wanted to date her. Around the end of the next semester, she started telling me that she felt weird about the whole situation, and it totally cooled off. Later that month, she told me that she cared deeply for me and was not quite sure what she wanted. We ended up at another dance, and I asked her to dance. She said that she did not feel like dancing, that she felt very tired. Two songs later, she was dancing with another guy, and the whole situation made me angry and frustrated. "Why won't she just tell me straight up?" I would lament to a good friend of mine while cruising in Lubbock. She then sent me an email saying that she felt really awkward around me despite the fact that she cared for me a lot. Satisfied with the closure, I went into the summer not feeling much of anything.

> "Always happens to my friends. It always happens to me. It's taken me nineteen years to finally see. She said, 'Can we just be friends? It's just not working out.' Another broken heart that I can do without."
> — "GSF," MXPX

One night on ICQ we began talking. The next night we talked again. The next night ... you get the idea. We started opening up our hearts to each other again, and it felt great. I even met her and her sister in Dallas for dinner one time. I visited her at her home another time. I was loving it. She came back to Lubbock in August and said that she could not wait until she saw me again. Despite my best efforts to contact her, that was the last I heard from her until I came back to Lubbock in the fall. Suffice it to say, I was frustrated and disappointed once again.

At this point, I gave up on her. I tried to put it out of my mind and move on with my life. Around Valentine's Day of the next semester we started talking again regularly. We decided to have an "anti-date." Honestly, at this point, I was fine with being just friends, but she went out of her way to tell me that she did not consider it a date and that it made her feel awkward. Fair enough. We parted ways again, and she left Lubbock and moved back home to go to school.

While I was home again that summer, she and I started talking again. She told me that she felt as if I were the only person she could confide in anymore because I had not turned my back on her. Feelings stirred up once again. She made a plan to come and stay at my parents' house for a couple of days so we could see each other and hang out. I was so excited. Finally, we were going to establish what should have happened a year ago. The only problem was that she got scared the morning she was supposed to come and did not show up. Needless to say, I was pretty bummed. She told me that she loved me, and I told her the same, but that I was confused and needed time to think. An upcoming two-week mission trip to Mexico would help clear my head. I told her that I would use that time away to consider it and pray about it. I kept getting a resounding "No!" while on the trip, and I told her as much when I got back. She was sad but understood.

Fast forward to September: she and I start talking again. I had gotten over it (more or less), but something about it felt so right that I fell into it again. But this time, I knew that nothing should happen. So, one night, I sent her an email (yes, an email) telling her that we should never talk again because it was bad for both of us to string it along. I did not hear anything from her the next day. The night after that, I got a phone call at 3:00 a.m. Not looking at the caller ID, I answered the phone. It was her. Here is the exact phone conversation:

Me: "Hello?"

Her: "Hey."

Me: "Uhhhh hey."

Her: "What are you doing?"

Me: "It's 3:00 a.m. I am sleeping."

Her: "Guess what?"

Me: "What?"

Her: "I'm in Lubbock."

OH.

NO.

Me: (a little hesitant) "Oh yeah?"

Her: "Yeah. Guess what else?"

Me: "What?"

Her: "I'm in your parking lot."

(awkward silence follows)

Her: "Are you going to come outside?"

I proceeded to go outside for a few minutes of awkwardness, then I mumbled something about needing to get some sleep and bade her good night.

The next day, like a chump, I did not answer my phone one time until she left for Dallas. I have not talked to her since.

The foundation for this book was laid when I began answering questions about relationships on my website, but my personal stake in this topic began as a young, immature freshman. About a month into answering reader emails, I received the inevitable question: "What should you do when you start to like a friend?" I answered it to the best of my ability and left it at that. Then another question came in about it. Then another one, from a different angle. Needless to say, this topic seemed to strike a chord with people. So, I decided to coin the term "friendlationship," which is basically the really awkward time where two friends are not quite sure whether or not they are dating. This is a very lively topic in the young adult Christian setting (probably because so many people kissed dating goodbye). Therefore, I have compiled a list of frequently asked questions about the Friendlationship issue.

What should you do when you start to like a friend? Everything becomes so confusing and complicated.

Yes, yes, yes. Who of us has not fallen prey to this situation? You hang out with a special person, a person that you consider an incredible friend, and then the possibilities start racing through your mind. "Why not us?" "I have been looking for love, and it has been staring me in the face for so long." You know the drill because you have thought these things before. All of a sudden that good friend becomes so much more to you, and you have no clue how to handle it. The funny thing is that it only becomes confused and complicated for you unless you tell this person how you feel. Any awkwardness that occurs is a result of you not quite knowing how to act around this person. After all, you were free to be yourself with them before: you could burp, tell stupid jokes, and be an all-around dork. We humans have a really strange mechanism that activates itself when we become attracted to somebody. Basically, it feeds us with the notion that we have to put our best face forward and not show any flaws. If we show people the absolute best we have (or at least hide the worst), we have a decent shot of attracting them. If this happens with someone you barely know, it is called flirting and showing interest in impressing the other person. When it occurs between two people who are already good friends, it is called, "What are you doing?" "Quit messing around!" and "Why are you so tense?" This mechanism is entirely ineffective in an already-established friendship. In fact, the use of that instinct in "established territory" is the primary cause of the perceived awkwardness and weirdness that inevitably come in these relationships.

So, there is the background of all of this awkwardness. Now, what do you do? The first thing to do is to objectively look at the chances of you two getting together. Do you have different long-term goals? Do you have differing ideas of what your personal ministry is going to be (i.e. missions in

Nepal versus teaching Sunday school in Dallas)? Another thing to consider is the qualities that this other person has that would lead to a positive relationship and/or detract from a positive relationship. Will this person, in a romantic relationship, lead you closer to God? Are you really falling for this person, or are you just feeling lonely and they are your most convenient way to end that loneliness? I suggest you spend at least one week away from that person seeking God's face. Is there something deficient in your relationship with Him that you are seeking somewhere else? I know from experience that I would develop feelings for a girl at the end of each semester. Very strange. Instead of trying to pursue this relationship at the last minute, I would take advantage of the month away and do a personal inventory of my spiritual life. Very often, asking the aforementioned questions gave me a peace of mind, and I was able to continue the positive friendship with her. These are all questions you need to be asking yourself.

Lloyd: I'm gonna take Diane Court out again.

Corey: Well, that's unlikely.

Lloyd: Is the movies a good second date? You know, as a date?

Corey: Well, you never had a first date.

Lloyd: Yes we did. I sat across from her at a mall. We ate together. We ate. That's eating, sharing an important physical event.

Corey: That's not even a scam.

Lloyd: What's a scam?

Corey: Going out as friends.
—SAY ANYTHING

If that does not work, tell another friend (someone who knows both of you but you can trust not to say/do anything about it) about your feelings. This person will be able to tell you if you are being irrational and will be able to keep you accountable with your actions. So, what if, after all of this, you still have feelings for this person? There is only one thing you can do: tell them. If you feel this strongly about this person, you owe it to yourself to share with them how you feel. This could very well end the friendship as you know it if they do not return the love, but it is a risk you have to take. If you push these feelings down, it will kill you whenever this person goes out with someone else. Take a chance. If they return the love, great; if not, it will be the impetus for you to begin moving on.

One thing to ask yourself is, "Why do you make friends with people of the opposite sex?" Are you solely looking for someone who might be "the one"? I know for a guy it is often easier to hang out with a girl he likes when they are friends than it is to ask her out. To become friends is a good thing, but it can also be used as a ploy to avoid the fears of asking someone out. Take a good look at the "friendships" you are forming. If they are solely to try to date someone, you need to check out your priorities.

But what do you do if you are the one that a friend has feelings for?

The first question that I have is, "How do you know for sure that this person has feelings for you?" Let us just assume that the other friend has not revealed their feelings toward you. What we are left with is a suspicion on your part that you might mean more to this person than any friend would. So, you think that their motives might be shifting. But you could be totally wrong. I know from personal experience that I have misinterpreted other women's kindness for flirtation or feelings. I think we have all had that bit of miscommunication at one time or another. So, how do you prevent this type of faux pas from occurring? Well, I do not recommend that you ask them flat out about their feelings toward you. More times than not, that will lead to instant denial. Such a direct question comes across as aggressive and often leads to the other person putting up a wall and growing defensive.

I remember when I was in fourth grade, I had a small crush on a girl in my class. So one day, she was sitting opposite me in the classroom and bluntly said, "So, Jeff, I hear you have a crush on me." My response? I shut down and hid behind my Pete Incaviglia folder for the rest of class. I did not even try to answer; I just could not.

You see, most of the time, the feelings that a friend might be developing for you are very awkward for them so they approach them very carefully. Sometimes at this point, they realize that they really do not have feelings for you specifically, it is just that they have a desire to be loved. If you approach them directly and do not give them a chance to sort their feelings out, they will never be able to be honest about it. To know for sure, you have to wait for them to tell you, or at least wait for them to drop obvious hints so that you can open the dialogue. Either way, wait for them to start the process. After all, at this point their feelings are the ones that have changed.

If there is a person who you know likes you more than a friend and you have been very honest about not feeling the same way toward them, can you still be friends?

One thing about this that needs to be realized is that as the one your friend happens to have romantic feelings for, you have an obligation to share your true feelings with them. Based on the question, this has been done, and you are wondering if the friendship has to suffer because a person's feelings grew deeper. Sadly, when a friendship changes to a crush, the friendship as you knew it dies. Things cannot be exactly the same anymore. When the view of the relationship changes for one person, the entire dynamic of the relationship is altered. After the talk has occurred and your feelings are known, it is best for you and your friend to not spend any significant amount of time together for a while. They are still probably struggling with their feelings, and they need to do some serious soul-searching once your feelings (or lack thereof) are made known. If you keep spending time with them during this period, they will (incorrectly) think that there is still an opportunity for you two to get together. It is not fair to toy with their emotions in this way. Please remember that although you just want to be friends, they do not; thus you need to respect their feelings and realize that you spending more and more time with them will only prevent them from coming to a resolution about their feelings for you. It is very difficult to get over somebody if you see them every day. So, give them their space and let them know that it is for their own good.

Next, you should not do anything that could be misconstrued as romantic. There are two types of motivations behind this behavior: innocent and "innocent." Innocent behaviors are those that you use to show your care and appreciation to all of your friends. Things such as hugs, words of love and affirmation, and physical touch may be normal in a relationship understood to be platonic, but if a person has a crush on you and you do these things, they will be viewed as flirting. You simply want to let them know you care; however, when they hear you say, "I care for you," they think, "I want to date you." That is simply the mentality that results from one friend having a crush on the other. Check your behavior and make sure that you are not keeping your friend from getting over this. "Innocence," on the other hand, is the duplicitous behavior that you use when you like knowing that someone has feelings for you. You hold someone's feelings hostage when you utilize the aforementioned behavior (hugs, words, etc.) to ensure that they still have feelings for you. If you are ever confronted about the behavior, you can simply say, "Oh, I just did that because you are my friend." If you are not ready to use them romantically, you can simply deny it and keep them in suspense. Proverbs 16:2 says, "All a man's ways seem innocent to him, but motives are weighed by the Lord." You are using your friend as a safety net to prevent you from facing your own feelings, and that leads to nothing but conflicted feelings on their part. Do yourself and them a favor, and adopt a Christlike attitude about the friendship.

When it comes down to it, whenever a person reveals their feelings to another, they are opening themselves up to mocking and ridicule. So you can imagine that when a friend reveals their feelings to another, they are taking a tremendous risk. As their friend, you need to treat their feelings with the utmost care and respect. Let them know how you truly feel and let them go. Hopefully, they will be able to return as your friend sometime down the line. Just do not try to rush things, and you should be fine. If they never want to be friends again, then either they are trying to protect themselves from feeling those things about you or they were only your friend in order to try to hook up with you. Either way, respect their decision and move on.

Why do my best friends of the opposite sex tell me, "I want to marry someone just like you"? Do they really want to marry me, or are they just saying it?

Here is my first bit of unpopular advice: you should not have a best friend of the opposite sex (hereby "OSF," or "opposite-sex friend") other than your significant other. It always leads to situations like this one where someone's feelings get hurt. I think the first question needs to be: "Do you have feelings for your best friend?" I am guessing "yes" because if he was just a friend to you, it probably would not bother you if he did not find you to be marriage material. But once again, the dangers of a close friendship without a DTR is that someone will get their feelings hurt. It is not always the girls, either. Guys say stuff like, "I wish I could marry you," and girls say things like, "I would not want to ruin our friendship." Either way, the person with the feelings gets hurt and feels rejected—even if you did not consciously reject them in any way.

I can think of two reasons why a friend would tell you, "I want to marry someone just like you." They suspect that you are developing feelings for them, or they really have feelings for you and are trying to see if you have feelings for them.

They suspect you are developing feelings for them.

Friends can almost always tell when their other friends have feelings for them. Their behavior will change, and they will act very awkwardly and try to hide it from them. If the guy in question thought that you might have feelings for him, but he does not see himself with feelings for you, then he may say something like that as a sort of preemptive strike in order to let you know how he feels without you

openly getting hurt about it. It may seem rude and hurtful, but he is trying to spare you the embarrassment (and
his own awkwardness about the situation) of realizing that
your professed love is unrequited. Guys can sympathize
with this one rather easily. Let's say that you are talking to a
girl you just met. She is gorgeous, and you are doing your
best to (not-so) subtly flirt with her. Since she automatically
recognizes this, she can casually mention her boyfriend in
a sentence and therefore prevent you from even asking her
out. It is a slick move that gives guys the hint every time.

Then there is the other guy. This guy says, "I want to marry
someone just like you," because he knows that you have
feelings for him. He tells you that so you may think you
have chance with him ("If he wants to marry someone like
me, maybe one day he will realize that he wants it to be
me") and keep your feelings for him afloat. Do you ever
watch *The Simpsons*? It is a known fact that Milhouse has a
crush on Lisa. One day she tells him that she is attracted to
a guy that reminds her of him. His response? "But I'm all
Milhouse! I'm the real thing!" The guy who employs this
tactic does so to satisfy his own relationship insecurities and
to use you as his fail-safe device; if he were ever crashing
and burning with another female, you would always be
there for him. The problem is that he may not even realize he is doing it. Every guy has some form of emotional
insecurities that he is not even totally aware that he has.
If you suspect a guy is doing that to you, go to a mutual
friend (male) and let him know of the situation. Then, he
can go and confront the other guy about it and see if they
can resolve this situation.

**They have feelings for you and want to know if you
have feelings for them.**

In this situation, the guy in question that says this really means, "I have feelings for you; there are so many qualities about you that I like, it's just that I am afraid of rejection, and I am afraid of how you would react if I told you how I really feel." This guy may be a little timid when it comes to initiating any type of romantic communication. It does not mean that he is a loser. It just means that he has been hurt before and is taking the first fragile steps out to let himself feel again. It is a low-risk way to see how you feel about the relationship. Either that, or he is trying to play a game and get you to share your feelings first. We must remember that these relationships are not games. When you get married, it becomes a picture of Christ's love for the Church. That is not a game, and it is not something to be taken lightly.

> "Better is open rebuke than hidden love."
> —PROVERBS 27:5

You see, passion is missing from the opposite-sex best friend relationship. The problem is that we have this preconceived notion of what the beginning stages of a romantic relationship are supposed to look like. In the fledgling stages, we are supposed to get to know the other person on a deeper level. If you already know them on a deep level, what is the point of developing feelings? You see the absolute worst in your opposite-sex best friend. There is no idealism to begin with, so I suppose it just does not feel right. People with this motivation forget the fact that love must develop into a choice and into a lifestyle, or the emotional "love" that new lovers feel will fade away, and you will be left with a shell of memories of yesterday.

The problem with this deep emotional involvement already there (and no definition of what the commitment or feelings are) is that you are setting yourselves up for failure. Guys, if you are going to give your heart to a girl, give it all to her. Do not hold anything back. If you form a committed relationship, you have a responsibility to serve her as Christ served the Church. If you hold something back, your relationship will always fall well short of the potential and plan that God has for it.

Would a guy friend of mine ask me if another female friend of mine was good-looking if he had feelings for me? In other words, would this be his way of saving you the embarrassment/his own awkwardness about the situation? I guess what it really comes down to is: How is a girl to know the difference between if a guy is "suspecting you have feelings for him" or if "he has feelings for you and wants to know if you have feelings for him also"?

I can only speak from personal experience about this one. Personally speaking, if I had a female friend who I had feelings for and I felt as if I were becoming attracted to her, I would not comment on any other ladies to her. If I thought I stood a reasonable chance of getting together with her, I would do everything in my power to make her feel as if she were the most important person in the world to me. If a guy really wants to pursue a relationship with you, he does not need to be playing games.

What is the point of playing games in relationships anyway? Each of us possesses real feelings and real hurts that we bring into the relationship. A common routine that people go through is "I just want to know if this person could have feelings for me," and then we freak out when they actually do. Playing games with someone's emotions is one of the most selfish, harmful, thoughtless acts you can perform. Remember, in a game, you have winners and losers. Nobody deserves to feel like a loser for having feelings for someone else.

Of course, there will be guys who joke around with you about other girls if they have feelings for you because they do not have any other method of handling potentially uncomfortable feelings. Boys will be boys, I suppose, but dealing with relationships is a man's game, and boys need not apply. That sounds harsh, but it is true: until you can deal with your own feelings, you will not be the partner that your SigOth needs you to be.

Finally, to know the difference, you basically need to have a DTR with the guy. If you think the situation is getting to the point where the friendship is either progressing to something more (if you both might have feelings) or falling away (if one of you is freaked out by the other's potential feelings), then communicate exactly how you feel. If you dance around the subject, the guy will feel like you were trying to lead him on that whole time when you were just trying to spare him the embarrassment of being turned down. In short, guys need to be told the truth in a firm yet caring way. We may not want it or like it, but if the message is unclear, we will always assume that the light is green.

I have a best friend who just got out of a serious relationship. I think I am developing feelings for him. What should I do?

Good question. I have a few of my own. How recent was his breakup? How long had he gone out with the other girl? If it was a very serious relationship that went on for a while, then he needs to take time off from dating relationships to heal and grow as an individual.

But once the time passes (or if it has already passed), how do you read him? It is difficult to say. He may be hard to read because he is nervous to let you know how he feels about you. Or he could be hard to read because he senses you might feel a certain way and it makes him uncomfortable because he does not. My best advice would be to keep encouraging him. Build him up and let him know that he can trust you with who he is. The more that you show you care for him, the more likely he will be to initiate a talk. A sign of a great woman is one who uses what she has to bring out the strength of a man. Let him feel safe to initiate, and he will if he is interested (in fact, he will probably think it was his own confidence that did it).

If you do all of these things and he is not interested, you need to ask yourself a couple questions. Can you still be his friend with these unrequited feelings? Are you putting too much in a friendship that is not leading in that direction?

How do I handle an opposite-sex best friend and a boyfriend/girlfriend?

It will never work. The SigOth will get jealous. If you are dating someone, they should be the most important person of that gender to you. If you give them less than that, you are not ready to be in a dating relationship. Eventually, one of you will get married and choose your spouse over the friend. If your spouse is to be your best friend and you do not plan on marrying your current best friend, then you need to step back and redefine the nature of your relationship. If you do not, one day someone's feelings will get hurt, and you will have several problems to rectify.

I was talking to a friend recently about a similar situation. He has a really solid OSF and has been dating this other girl for a few months. The only problem is that his way of asking girls out is to become friends with them first. Now he is not sure how to handle his OSF (whom he has had unconscious feelings for) and his girlfriend. I asked him who he would choose if it came down to it, and he said he would choose the OSF because "[their] friendship is worth too much to throw away." But the problem is that he does not value the friendship, only the potential romantic relationship that is there; he does not want to burn his bridges. He needs his OSF as an emotional parachute in case things go awry with his girlfriend. Personally, I do not think he should have ever jumped out of the plane.

My main problem with friendlationships is that they are dangerous. Hurt and confusion are inevitable in a relationship without clear direction. We owe it to ourselves and to our brothers and sisters in Christ to be honest and open with each other. Stop pretending you are playing *The Sims*. This is real life with real people with real problems. Start living it intentionally.

Oh yeah, and don't break off a relationship via email.

CHAPTER FOUR

SINGLES SATISFACTION AND THE COUPLES CULTURE

Meet Ashley. Ashley is very active in her church and is always willing to lend a helping hand to others. She has a great heart and desires to change lives. Ashley has always had a boyfriend. I do not mean that she has been dating the same guy, but she has had boyfriends steadily since adolescence. After she breaks up with a guy, she immediately begins looking for another one. She was telling me one day how she was tired of being with horrible guys. I suggested that she take a break from dating so that she could clear her head and know exactly what she wants. My suggestion puzzled her as she replied, "You don't understand. I can't not have a boyfriend. I would be too lonely."

Things like this happen when a person does not find satisfaction as a single person. If you are looking for absolute fulfillment in another person, you are setting yourself up for failure. I heard a man once say, "If you cannot find peace in yourself, it is futile to search for it elsewhere." You have to be satisfied with your identity as a single person; you have to have a developing, growing relationship with Christ, or you will not be well suited for a relationship. In 1 Corinthians, Paul shares some insight about the benefits of finding Singles Satisfaction.

"Now to the unmarried and the widows I say: It is good for them to stay unmarried, as I am" (1 Cor. 7:8). In chapter 7, Paul shares his opinion about the benefits of being single. Having never been married, Paul was able to find peace in God and satisfaction in being single. Throughout the chapter, Paul breaks down several benefits for being single and offers insight into finding the elusive Singles Satisfaction.

"Brothers, each man, as responsible to God, should remain in the situation God called him to." (1 Cor. 7:24)

Translation: Accept the fact that you might never get married.

Does this mean you should never look for a spouse? Of course not. It means that, for some of you, God might be calling you to be single for your entire life. If you stray outside of God's calling, then you are setting yourself up for heartache and misery. You will be trading true love for a fake, for a lust of the world that will leave you beaten and disenfranchised. If being in a dating relationship is your number one goal, you need to rethink your life's direction. Your lot in life is not to be in a relationship—it is to honor and glorify God. You need to view being single as a blessing and trust God's plan for your life. Most of you will get married, but some of you will not. Is that fair? It is not for me to say. I am merely telling you that allowing yourself to feel these feelings and basing your whole life around hooking up with someone leads to nothing but emptiness.

"Are you married? Do not seek a divorce. Are you unmarried? Do not look for a wife." (1 Cor. 7:27)

Translation: Do not date someone for the sake of dating.

By all means, keep your eyes open, but do not assume that because there is a mutual attraction with a person, you need to be in a relationship. You must assess the situation and circumstances realistically and, above all else, pray about it. As a believer, you are not above becoming attracted to a non-Christian or a married person (see chapter 5). Also, do not simply date out of boredom. Dating, in the sense that I have defined it, is an intentional decision utilized to determine romantic possibilities. Anything done out of boredom does not imply a desire to love someone else, but a desire to remove the boredom by using the other person. You may be bored and want to date someone because you have nothing better to do. The person you are on the date with may already be planning the wedding. Feelings have a tendency to spring up when two people spend a lot of time together. If you are with the person for your own comfort, then you are dating for the wrong reasons. You need to date somebody because you love them and they love you. Pity and boredom have no place in establishing a dating relationship.

"I would like you to be free from concern. An unmarried man is

concerned about the Lord's affairs—how he can please the Lord.
But a married man is concerned about the affairs of this world—
how he can please his wife—and his interests are divided. An
unmarried woman or virgin is concerned about the Lord's affairs:
Her aim is to be devoted to the Lord in both body and spirit. But
a married woman is concerned about the affairs of this world—how
she can please her husband. I am saying this for your own good,
not to restrict you, but that you may live in a right way in undi-
vided devotion to the Lord." (1 Cor. 7:32-35)

**Translation: Instead of praying for God to bring you
the right person, pray that God will make you the
right person.**

In marriage (and dating) the temptation is strong to have
your interests divided. If you think it is difficult to spend
time praying and reading God's Word as a single person,
wait until you have a physical person there with whom you
want to spend every waking
moment. If you think you
have a strong resistance to
premarital sex, be prepared to
resist the strongest desires you
have ever felt while looking in
the eyes of the most beautiful person who has the exact
same desires as you. Ideas about how to do well in relationships are overrun by actions in a hurry. Being in a relationship is a big responsibility that is not for the faint of heart.
Every person in the world wants to marry someone who is
awesome, sweet, and outstanding. Are you asking God each
day to improve your character? Remember that a relationship is not just about how you benefit from the other person; it is about how you can invest in that person's life for

"Resistance is futile.
Individualism is irrelevant."

*—THE BORG,
STAR TREK: THE
NEXT GENERATION*

the better. On another note, pray that God will make you the right person for the sake of honoring Him and not to attract others to you. God will do very little for you if your concern is not for His glory.

"Now about virgins: I have no command from the Lord, but I give a judgment as one who by the Lord's mercy is trustworthy. Because of the present crisis, I think that it is good for you to remain as you are. Are you married? Do not seek a divorce. Are you unmarried? Do not look for a wife. But if you do marry, you have not sinned; and if a virgin marries, she has not sinned. But those who marry will face many troubles in this life, and I want to spare you this." (1 Cor. 7:25-28)

Translation: Realize that not everything in a relationship is wine and roses.

Your problems do not go away when you get into a relationship. In fact, you still have the same problems you always had, and now you get to experience your SigOth's problems as well (see chapter 6). Your problems are multiplied, but you have the benefit of working through them with someone you love. In real life, happily ever after is a pipe dream that is scoffed at by anyone who actually, you know, lives on this planet.

Look inside and see what feelings are there that you should so strongly desire a relationship. Is your relationship with God where it should be? Often, we misinterpret our faltering relationship for God as an act of loneliness and need for human companionship. Have you been spending time in prayer? Is there something that God has been speaking to you about and you have been ignoring? I feel one problem with our generation is that it is too easy to get in contact with other people. Sometimes we just need the moments of isolation where we get to wrestle with God and ourselves. We do not always need to talk to other people when things are going badly. If you find an overwhelming desire to be with someone, then you might want to consider spending time alone, just you and God, to sort out your relationship. We try to fill too many things in the holes of our relationship with God: boyfriends, girlfriends, television, money, sex, alcohol, emotional experiences. Until your relationship with God is where it needs to be, you will not be as effective in a relationship as you can be.

Do you come to church to worship God or to meet people of the opposite sex?

When I got home from work the other day, I was flipping through the channels and landed on *Elimidate*. As with a horrific car crash, I was compelled to watch. The guy was down to choosing between two girls. He asked them if they would stay home when he went to the clubs or if they were going to join him. That made me think: if this guy were to enter a serious relationship with one of these ladies, the bars or clubs would not be as exciting. He was using the club scene as a means to an end (to hook up with somebody). The clubs would lose their charm if he had already "hooked up." I know, I know. What does this have to do with us?

Maybe more than you realize.

Replace "club" or "bar" with "church." Are you merely going to church because you want to hook up with a good Christian person of the opposite sex? Is your joy in worship because God is awesome or because that cute guy/girl smiled and waved at you? You might find that once you get into a relationship, church does not feel like it did when you were single. Maybe it is because you used church as a means to an end. It was a "good" bar or a "moral" club, but it was still used the same way.

I have heard a lot of talk about people who do not come to church for the "right reasons." Some think they should not come if their heart is not ready; others think that it does not matter because it makes the sanctuary look full; still others think that these are the exact people who need to hear the truth of God's love. I am not presently concerned with "those people," nor should you be. All we can do is make sure that our hearts are ready, that our motives are pure. Use church as a time to encounter God and be encouraged, and you might meet a dateable person. But if you go to church to meet a dateable person, you will neither establish a great relationship or encounter God.

> "If we are incapable of finding peace in ourselves, it is pointless to search elsewhere."
> —FRANCOIS DE LA ROCHEFOUCAULD

The necessity of finding Singles Satisfaction cannot be stressed enough. If you are not careful with your spiritual life as a single person, you might fall into The Couples CULTure.

What? You mean you have never heard of The Couples CULTure? Read on.

THE COUPLES CULTure

Meet Joe. Joe has three really close friends, and he does everything with them. They hang out all the time and have been compared to a band of brothers. Then Joe meets "her."

Guys, you know what I am talking about. She is cute, but not good-looking enough for Joe; she is nice, but not nice enough. After all, Joe desires a girl who is incredible, and this girl, well, she is just mediocre from your point of view. The problem is, however, that he really likes her. No, he really, really likes her. He likes her so much, in fact, that you hardly ever see him anymore. He spends all of his time with her, and the little time he spends with you is awkward because he is looking at you through the lens of "we-ness" (i.e. "WE do not like to eat Chinese food" or "We cannot go out because we always watch *Felicity* together"). You can even tell that he secretly pities you because of your singles solitude. Then, the realization hits: "Dear God, he has been infected by The Couples CULTure! He is one of them!"

The Couples CULTure is a group of couples who seek to separate themselves from the rest of society and hang out with others just like them. You can deduce their association with this group by their innate desire to be defined solely by their relationship. In essence, it would appear to those who knew the individuals BH (Before Him/Her) that they have lost all sense of self and identity. That is the stigma of couple-hood. These days, many couples are viewed the same way; as they begin a relationship, they forsake their own individual identities for the chance of acceptance. This is not always the case, but The Couples CULTure is doing nothing to hinder the stereotype. In fact, if you are different from those in The Couples CULTure, they will either ignore you or attempt to have you join and become "one of them." Couples get a bad rap, and I think I know why.

The truth must be revealed.

We have all been in situations where we are hanging out

by ourselves with a couple that does not seem to know you exist. They are so "into each other" that you are barely a blip on their radar. Any conversation you make somehow ties into the love they have for each other or is soundly ignored while they stare lovingly into each other's eyes. It looks like "true love," when in fact it is rude and disrespectful to the other person. "That will never be me," many people state until they are assimilated.

You do have a choice.

Do not be fooled by the wedding band on my finger or the marriage license with my name on it. Alison and I utterly refuse to take part in that CULTure and have been ostracized. We are fine with that; after all, we strive for unity not uniformity. But some of you are in The Couples CULTure without even realizing it. Now, I would like to give you a few warning signs that you, my friend, might be taking part in The Couples CULTure.

1) Another couple instantly becomes your new best friends.

After all, single people can never relate to you anymore. Only couples can! You must be friends with a couple first and foremost. Why is this? You do not instantly become another person as soon as you are in a relationship, unless you are in The Couples CULTure. Your single friends are still your friends. Being in a relationship does not change that. For a short while Alison and I tried to find couples with which to hang out and spend time. Many couples we encountered were dull as dirt because they were too into each other. It was impossible for us to relate to them because all they knew (and frankly, all they wanted to know) was each other. They had their own little world and were content to be oblivious to everyone else. There was no way they could invest in us or help us grow, and it was very unlikely they wanted to be invested in either. After all, they had each other. I do not know if you ever listen to other people's conversations, but a pair of couples that are best friends have some of the dullest conversation you can imagine. Everything is funny and/or wacky. Think about your friendships. Where are your single friends? Do you have difficulties identifying with them now?

2) You become increasingly awkward around single people.

If you are having problems being around single people, you have a problem. Being awkward with singles and embracing couples you barely know is a vicious cycle. Again, there is no need for awkwardness around single people. They do not need your pity for being single; they need you to be their friend. Throughout my life I have had many good friends who disappear the second they get a girlfriend. Then when

> "Now to the unmarried and the widows I say: It is good for them to stay unmarried, as I am."
> —1 CORINTHIANS 7:8

they would make time to hang out with me, it was very weird. I have a friend who used to play me in Nintendo 64's *Goldeneye 007* all the time. It is a very fun game, and he and I would have a blast. As usual, I was dominating. (Trevelyan. Grenade Launchers. Temple. If you have the guts.) After his sound defeat, he looked at me and said, "It's fine. You won this game. Now, I'm just gonna go hang out with my girlfriend. You know, since I actually have one." (Note: This type of trash talking is typical among guys and is also grounds for a beating.)

Seriously, rappers have shot each other for this kind of talk.) You see, the joke belied a hidden truth. He felt as if he was lowering himself to play me in a video game. After all, he had a girlfriend; he had no more use for me. Anyway, she dumped him a month later. I even let him win a game of *Goldeneye*. Yeah, right. I am not that empathetic. My point is that your single friends still have value and are still people. Choose to be their friend, not their object of mockery and "why doesn't she spend time with us anymore, that jerk" conversations.

3) You ask permission to do things.

"I do not know if I can hang out or not. I will have to see if it is OK with him." Ouch. Remember when I said that in a dating relationship, the date is implied? True, a date is implied, but spending every spare moment with your SigOth is not. It is actually healthy for you two to do things apart from one another regularly (as long as it is not harmful to the relationship). You are not married yet. You are not joined at the heart, so there is no need to be joined at the hip either. You do not have to ask permission to do anything. Of course, you need to show consideration, but there is a fine line between showing consideration and acting whipped. This applies to guys and girls alike. It is not, "I need to check with her and see if it is OK." It is either, "Of course, let me call and let her know," or "Well, I would love to, but I already have plans." Make your time together a priority, but also respect each other's need for time apart.

4) You feel the need to proselytize all of your single friends into The Couples CULTure.

In other words, you try to hook everybody up. Don't both-

er. It is not your responsibility to put everyone in a relationship. Resist the temptation. After all, if you try to fix your
single friends up, it confirms the fact that you have pity on
them and that their life will not have meaning unless they
are in a relationship. That is inaccurate and hurtful. It is wise
to not transfer your insecurities onto others.

5) Your spiritual life is dependent on your SigOth's attitude.

Remember the earlier statement about taking joy in a worship service because you felt you received approval from the
person you had your eye on? This is what happens when
you leave that problem unchecked. You find yourself spiritually dry because your SigOth happens to be in a bad mood.
I have known dating couples who, if one person was sick
and unable to attend church, the other would not attend either. In a marital relationship that is often necessary in order
to help with housework and whatnot, but in a dating relationship it is not needed. You do not go to heaven in pairs.

If any of these apply to you, you have my pity. But all is not
lost. There are many things that you can do to prevent finding your identity in someone else. One thing that you need
to do is take at least one day a week off from each other.
This gives you time to be alone and work on things that
need attention. It also gives you a chance to hang out with
your single friends who you may not get to see as much.
Every person needs people of the same gender with whom
to identify and encourage.

You also need to spend serious time working on your
relationship with God. Is something lacking with God that
you feel the need to look for in someone else? There might

be some serious soul-work to do. Spend time intentionally building your relationship with Christ. The more you do this, the better SigOth you will become.

We do not achieve our "destiny" by being in a relationship. That is not our goal. Our goal is to grow closer and love God; you can do this as a single person or as one in a relationship. The people around us will all die someday; if we allow ourselves to be defined by them, then where does that leave us when they are gone?

People in The Couples CULTure hate being single. They utterly hate being alone and feel as if their happiness is defined by true love. Is it wrong to desire a relationship? No. Should that be your desire above all others? Absolutely not. Find peace in God, not in others.

Oh yeah, and don't bring SigOths into your video game trash-talking.

CHAPTER FIVE
SO YOU LIKE AN UNTOUCHABLE ...

Meet Jim. Jim just came to a new church as a freshman in college and is looking to make new friends. He sees her across the room; she has a beautiful smile, stunning eyes, and a wonderful presence. More importantly, the girl with whom she was just talking has walked away; Molly is standing all by herself. "This is it," thinks Jim. "This is my chance." He strolls over to meet her, and they carry on a really great conversation. All of the time, in the back of his mind, Jim is attempting to build up the courage to ask Molly for her phone number.

She tells him, "We really need to hang out sometime."

He replies, "That would be awesome," getting ready to make his move.

"Yeah, it would; I think you and my boyfriend would get along really well."

Awkward silence.

"You, you have a b-boyfriend?"

Jim kicks himself because he was just drawn into the temptation of the untouchable. The untouchable is "a person you are attracted to who is already in a relationship" or "a person you are attracted to other than your SigOth." We have heard these stories our whole lives. Alanis Morissette references "meeting the man of [her] dreams and then meeting his beautiful wife" ("Ironic"). Liz Phair tempts a guy with a girlfriend with the burning question, "What if this is just the beginning?" ("Why Can't I"). Look around you; chances are you will see a plethora of songs and media dedicated to this love for someone who is off limits. We are inculcated with these messages every day. Go to a theater and at least two of the movies deal with this. Reese Witherspoon, Sandra Bullock, and others have made a significant amount of money exploiting this desire. The media influences therein feed us false stereotypes and leave us broken and confused.

After all, in *Titanic*, Rose is not supposed to marry Cal, she is supposed to be with Jack, albeit briefly. You see, one of the constants in Hollywood is that the person in a relationship who is attracted to an untouchable is almost always in a relationship with someone who is abusive and evil. And in the end, "true love" wins out, and everyone lives happily ever after. Or not. Life rarely follows art in this way. There is never a happily ever after as long as we are breathing. We have to live with the choices we make and the people we make the choices about.

So why do we allow ourselves to absorb these unrealistic views on relationships? I do not want to sit here and blame this all on the media and on "the world." In fact, I feel that these messages fed to us by the media are merely mirroring our own fallen desires. We misplace our desire and feel that if we are attracted to an untouchable, we have to act upon it. One time, I heard someone say, *"I've learned in my lifetime so far that you can't help who you fall for."*

Is that a fact? I personally believe that statement to be full of fluff and deceit. It is a cop-out to let our heart totally rule our lives, to the exclusion of our mind and soul. Any decision that we make with regard to love should include all three. After all, the greatest commandment is that we love God with all our heart, all our soul, and our entire mind (Mark 12:30). Since our earthly love is a picture of our relationship with God, it needs to be the same. To let one aspect of our being outrule the rest is dangerous and unhealthy. It leads us down a path to an unbalanced life where we are slaves to our desires.

If you think that this temptation does not exist in the Church, then you need to educate yourself. During my freshman year of college, we went on a spring break mission trip to Southern California. Shortly after the trip, one of the churches we helped had an explosion in attendance. There was an all-around larger interest in God in the area.

Basically, the church was experiencing revival. Within a year, however, the pastor (with whom I had the opportunity to speak on a few occasions) resigned and got a divorce. He and his secretary ran off together after beginning an illicit relationship. These stories are not at all uncommon. Being under the blood of Christ does not exempt us from making foolish decisions that can ruin our lives.

> "Cheers, darlin', here's to you and your lover man."
>
> —*"CHEERS DARLIN',"*
> *DAMIEN RICE*

But why are untouchables even an issue? Does the fact that they are restricted make them so tantalizing? Do we only want that which we are not supposed to have? Is there any logical reason why relationships with untouchables should be pursued? No. But those looking for relationships have set their hearts above all else in a desperate attempt to find that storybook romance, not caring about the feelings of those they have to step on to get there.

Dealing with the untouchables is like walking in a land mine of broken hearts and empty promises. To properly analyze the danger, we must look at each definition of the untouchable and address the issues therein.

You are attracted to someone who is already in a relationship.

Jim's situation is a typical one. Every guy reading this has tried to ask a girl out without noticing the engagement ring on her left hand or realizing that she is taken. It is an embarrassing situation that leaves both men and women frustrated. At this point, Jim should give up pursuing her because she is perfectly happy in her relationship.

"But what if Molly was in a horrible relationship?"

If you found yourself asking that question, pat yourself on the back. You win the Most Obvious, Desperate Question Asked to Yourself While Reading a Book by Jeff Taylor Award. To be fair, I knew some of you would ask that question. Why do I find myself trying to ask it as well? This question shows that we have an intense desire for our feelings to be validated and reciprocated, no matter what. I will address each part in turn and show you why it is unwise to act in either situation.

The person is in a healthy relationship.

If the person is in a healthy relationship, do absolutely nothing. You may like them, but so what? The relationship that they have is working well, and you need to leave it alone so that it can grow into something truly special. If you really care about this person, then you want them to be happy, and a positive relationship will make them happy. But if you superficially say, "I want them to be happy," but secretly think, "as long as it is with me," then you are acting out of selfishness and a lack of self-confidence. In this situation, loving them has nothing to do with your motivation; you are motivated by a desire for them to love you. Look deep into yourself and see what your intentions are in any relationship. If you are just taking feelings from people to feel better, you are an emotional dependent who needs to learn to respect himself and respect other people's feelings as well. Commitments need to be honored. If you were in a relationship, you would want someone else to respect the commitments you have made. Therefore, you do not have the right to disrupt a healthy relationship.

The person is in an unhealthy relationship.

If the person is in an unhealthy relationship, you will find
yourself in a bind. Yes, it is healthy to want them to be happy and away from the negative relationship, but you should
not help them break off that relationship with the intention of forming your own. You are not the hero. You are not
their savior. You will not swoop down and rescue them and
ride off into the sunset. It simply will not work. Did you
ever wonder why counselors are not allowed to date their
clients? It is because adding strong feelings to a counseling
session leads to disaster. Your motives would not be pure,
and neither your mind nor theirs would be clear. The last
thing that a person needs when coming out of a lengthy
relationship (good or bad) is another relationship. They
need to take a hiatus of at least six months from any and
all romantic relationships in order to deal with their pain
and feelings and grow as an individual. Why is the rebound
relationship treated like a joke? Because everyone knows
it will not last. The person on the rebound is just trying to
avoid sorting out their feelings by themselves and is refusing
to give it to God. The break is necessary, and we need to let
God heal the pain and hurt before moving on.

**You're in a relationship, but you cannot stop think-
ing about this other person.**

What do you do? Well, if you're willing to break up with
the love of your life at the first signs of attraction to someone else, then you will find yourself in a steady cycle of
attraction and boredom until the next attraction comes. If
you have to break up with your partner, make sure that you
are doing so for the right reason (i.e. you two don't fit together) and not because you like someone else. In order to

guard yourself from this, you need to follow the aforementioned hiatus of at least six months. Those six months will help keep your priorities in perspective. But confusion with regard to priorities can come in, mainly from a mix of our own sinful nature and the messages fed to us from the outside. The main problem with media influences (i.e. *Titanic*) is that we subconsciously internalize the idea of "current partner = villain" and view our partner as evil when we become attracted to someone else. This is a blatant lie, and it needs to be treated as such.

Now then, I am about to lose my guy card (with all grilling privileges), but there is a movie that properly (to an extent) addresses the realities of the untouchable. That movie is *Forces of Nature*. Ben Affleck plays a guy named Ben (how original) who gets stranded on the way to his wedding and falls in with a free-spirited woman named Sarah (Sandra Bullock) who offers to accompany him on his journey. As they get closer to the wedding, Ben finds himself falling in love with Sarah. She is very attractive and generates feelings in him that have long been dormant. He begins to question whether or not he really wants to marry his fiancée. When they arrive on the day of the wedding, he sees his fiancée and remembers exactly why he wanted to marry her. As the couple recites their vows, Sarah fades into the background and out of their lives. At the moment of reuniting with his bride, Ben has these thoughts:

> *[I thought that] when you found that [special] person, the rest of the world just kind of magically faded away, and, you know, the two of you would just be inside this kind of protective bubble. But there is no bubble or, if there is, we have to make it.*

You see, Ben was inundated with the thoughts of happily ever after. He thought that true love would not take any work, that the pressures and temptations of the world around them would just bounce off and have no effect. But he learned that if you want to protect your relationship, intense effort is involved. If your SigOth is worth it, you will go out of your way to stay loyal and true.

There is another movie that deals with this problematic issue in a realistic manner. *The Good Girl*, starring Jennifer Aniston, is a look at a young woman in small-town America who has a dead-end job, a pot-smoking husband, and a general lack of joy. Aniston plays a woman by the name of Justine who feels as if her life is headed nowhere.

> *As a girl you see the world as a giant candy store filled with sweet candy and such. But one day you look around, and you see a prison and you're on death row. You want to run or scream or cry, but something's locking you up. Are the other folks … just keeping quiet like you, planning their escape?*

She is miserable and wants out. Her husband is constantly stoned and wrapped up in pity and self-loathing. He is so caught up in his problems that he ignores the problems of his wife to the point that she feels unloved. In his Song of Solomon conference, Tommy Nelson likes to tell guys that if they do not tell their wife that they love her, then Satan will send someone who will. In this instance, Justine meets Holden, a stock boy at her place of work who enjoys writing. He is younger than her, enigmatic, and intriguing. Feelings stir within her, and soon enough she is spending more time with him, culminating in an affair.

Her justification is that this is her best chance to get away. She does not want to go to her grave with unlived life in her veins. She feels as if she is dying and has a need for freedom, a need to scream from the mountaintops, "I'm alive!" Everything seems perfect. It all makes sense now. He would regularly write stories for her.

> *[His stories] were about a girl who was put upon, whose job is like a prison, and whose life has lost all meaning. Other people do not get her, especially her husband. One day she meets a boy who is also put upon, and they fall in love. After spending their whole lives never getting got, with one look, they get each other completely.*

The ultimate fairy tale. Slap Fabio on the cover, and you would have a Harlequin bestseller. She feels important, understood, and loved (maybe). She starts contemplating the possibility of this story becoming true for her and Holden one day. One day, it happens. Holden makes a proposition for her to leave everything behind and join him (or "follow her heart") and truly live life. It comes down to her deciding whether or not to meet him at the hotel or go to her job that day, business as usual.

> "Holding hands with you when we're out at night. Got a girlfriend, you say it isn't right. And I've got someone waiting too. What if this is just the beginning? We're already wet, and we're gonna go swimming."
>
> —"WHY CAN'T I,"
> LIZ PHAIR

> *How it all came down to this, only the devil knows. Retail Rodeo is at the corner on my left. The motel is down the road to my right. I close my eyes and try to peer into the future. On my left, I saw days upon days of lipstick*

and ticking clocks, dirty looks, and quiet whisperings. And burning secrets that just won't ever die away. And on my right, what could I picture? The blue sky, the desert earth, stretching out into the eerie infinity. A beautiful neverending nothing.

The choice seems obvious; she has finally decided to make her escape to live life like she is destined. But she ultimately decides to go to work and renew her commitment to her husband. He forgives her for the affair, and they take the first trembling steps on the road to marital recovery.

> "When we meet someone beautiful and clever and sympathetic, of course we ought, in one sense, to admire and love these good qualities. But is it not very largely in our own choice whether this love shall, or shall not, turn into what we call 'being in love'?"
>
> *—MERE CHRISTIANITY,*
> *C.S. LEWIS*

It is by no means the typical ending for a movie. But you know, there is no reason for us to expect a Hollywood ending in any of our lives. The other person who is scorned does not simply fade away. They carry the pain and trauma of it all for the rest of their lives. There is a reason that Jesus said that marital unfaithfulness was the only reason for divorce; it violates a sacred, holy trust and is next to impossible to overcome. Again the world tries to excuse this behavior in typical fashion. The song "21 Questions" by 50 Cent says, *"If I was with some other chick and someone happened to see, and you asked me about it, I said it wasn't me. Would you believe me? Or up and leave me? How deep is our bond if that's all it takes for you to be gone?"* When I first heard this song, I could not help but laugh. The concept was ludicrous. The girl leaves 50 (or "Fiddy," if you prefer) because of his unfaithfulness.

Yet *he* questions *her* commitment to the relationship. The more I think about it, the more I realize just how sad this perspective is. Unfaithfulness is not a trite issue. Marriage (and its younger cousin, dating) are commitments that should be treated with utmost respect.

However, this does not change the fact that you may develop initial feelings for another person. We are creatures designed to love, but our designs have been corrupted, so our love, in the romantic sense, can sometimes be misplaced. You need to realize that it is totally natural to be attracted to someone else, but it is harmful and unnatural for you to act on it if you have already made a commitment. Do not beat yourself up for falling into that trap; just get yourself out of it.

So how do you do that exactly?

I recommend that you spend extra time with your SigOth and remember why you chose to be with them in the first place. There must have been some incredible qualities that attracted you to begin with. There is a reason why you are with your SigOth; spend serious time thinking about them and praying for them. You see, we can let these intense surface emotions for others cloud our judgment for our partner. Remember why you loved them and chose to be with them and get back to doing it. Decide to love them again.

The problem, however, is not totally averted yet. Once you decide to stick with your current partner despite the feelings you have for the other person, you have one major rule to follow: never spend time alone with the other person. Ever. This can lead to conflicted feelings and unfortunate circumstances. It is much easier to forgive a boyfriend/girlfriend for thinking someone else is attractive; it is much harder to forgive them if they have already sowed the seeds of a relationship with the untouchable.

So the next question is, "Do I have to forgive them for wanting to be with someone else?" The answer is "yes." You do have to forgive them. But forgiving them does not mean that you have to stay in the relationship with them. Each case is unique, however. Part of me wants to say that I would break it off with Alison if she cheated on me. But the other part, that pesky conscience, tells me that I should try to work it out with her. I will say this, though. If you develop a root of bitterness (not hurt) toward them, then it is in each of your best interests to end the relationship immediately. It is impossible to love someone with bitterness in your heart. But if your SigOth is penitent and desires to renew their commitment to you, then give it a shot. Mistakes happen. But when the same mistake keeps happening over and over again (when the person is a slave to their desire), you might need to get out of the relationship (see chapter 6 for more).

As long as we are in this world, we must learn to keep our fallen desires in check. Let your heart, mind, and soul work together to effectively love others. Listening to the heart alone can be deceptive; guard your heart with everything you've got (Prov. 4:23).

Oh yeah, and check Molly's left hand before asking her out.

CHAPTER SIX

BAGGAGE BASICS

Meet Abigail. Abigail is a pretty, charismatic girl with a lot going for her. She is an active leader in the church and helps mentor and disciple several younger ladies. She never meets a stranger and is kind and compassionate to everyone. Speaking with her and seeing her life now, you would never believe the things that Jesus Christ has washed away in her life. She was once addicted to drugs. She has had an eating disorder. She has struggled with depression and anxiety for years. At one point in her relationship with an emotionally abusive boyfriend, she became pregnant. She decided to have an abortion. Her old life was one of pain, isolation, and despair. You see, the blood of Christ did, indeed, cleanse her of her sins, but her memories of her old life will be there forever.

With that story in mind, I am going to give you a list of issues and problems that people face. I want you to tell me which of these apply to Christians and which ones do not. Here is but a sample of the pain in the world:

- Depression
- Abuse
- Chemical addiction
- Gambling addiction
- Pornographic addiction
- Attention Deficit Disorder
- Crippling injury
- Mental retardation
- Pain from a previous relationship
- Homosexuality
- Self-hatred
- Oppositional Defiant Disorder
- Antisocial Personality Disorder
- Greed

If you found yourself excluding any of these from people in the Church, think again. At one point, we were all sinners, and there is not a single one of us who does not feel the pain of loss, sadness, or betrayal. The fact that our sins have been washed away does not negate the reality of their occurrence. We all have scars from pain inflicted upon us by others and by ourselves. These are the factors that lead to problems in relationships.

You see, as humans, we all have certain quirky idiosyncrasies that set us apart from everyone else. One by one, these qualities are revealed in a relationship. As each person gets to know the other, the level of intimacy deepens, and we learn details about each of our lives. When the baggage is uncovered or revealed, it is time to decide to work with your SigOth through the problem or to walk away from them. The problems cannot be ignored. Generally speaking, baggage falls into two distinct categories: the Ugly and the Bad.

The ugly aspects are the traits that a person can do nothing about. There are hundreds of potentially awkward traits that we possess. You are able to identify most of yours, and if you are dating, you can probably identify your SigOth's as well. These traits are not cute, and they are not pleasant. Your pet peeves and their bad habits often interact in the ugly area as well as oil and water. Issues like AD/HD, mental health problems, or even crooked teeth are real problems regardless of the intentions of the person who has them. But it is not healthy or fair to hold them against your SigOth because there is precious little that can be done about them. Do not ask someone to change things that they are incapable of changing. It adds unneeded stress to the relationship and can result in them not trusting you as much as they should. It is hard to trust somebody if they do not accept and understand you. C.S. Lewis discusses this in *Mere Christianity:* "The bad psychological material is not a sin but a disease. It does not need to be repented of, but to be cured." Do not confuse issues of taste with issues of morality. When that confusion occurs, witch hunts tend to follow.

The bad characteristics, on the other hand, are the result of negative decisions made by an individual. Abusive behavior, a demeaning attitude, etc. are all classified as bad. These are things a person does with full intention and motivation. Theologically speaking, these are the sins of the will, things that a person has the option to choose against. Since we all have flaws in this area that we struggle with, we utilize the accountability aspect of a relationship to deal with these things. If you see your partner doing things that you know are wrong, it is up to you to lovingly rebuke them. Remember to do so with gentleness and respect (1 Pet. 3:15). If accountability is ignored or scoffed at, break up with that person as soon as possible. It would just be a matter of time before they turn their negative attitude and behavior against you as well.

Consequently, there are two types of people who carry the bad baggage. The first is someone who is bound to these things and continues to do them with no thought of conscience as to whether it is right or wrong. The other is someone who is working to overcome these problems. Whichever group you belong to (and all of us belong to one or the other), you must realize that you will probably find yourself in a relationship someday. You will have to deal with these issues in yourself and, as importantly, in your SigOth.

In order to establish the work that is set before you, let me give you another story. This story is not real, in the sense that these events specifically happened to an actual person, but I feel it represents the plight of Baggage Basics as well as any other. It is probably especially familiar to you Tom Hanks fans.

Meet Jenny. Jenny is an intelligent and caring young lady from Alabama. But Jenny has problems. You see, when Jenny was a child, her father sexually molested her constantly. One day, he was arrested, and she lived with her grandma. After high school, she moved to an all-female college where she dated different guys all of the time. One evening, her simple-minded friend from high school catches her boyfriend trying to do things to her and attacks him. That night, she tries to sleep with this simple-minded friend. He freaks out, and nothing happens. Later, Jenny is seen in *Playboy* posing provocatively in her college sweater, causing her expulsion from school.

She then takes a job at a strip club and, one evening, gets in trouble, and her simple-minded friend is there to rescue her, once again. She chastises him and tells him that she is leaving. Later, Jenny falls into the free love movement and starts abusing drugs and sleeping with abusive boyfriends. At one point, she even contemplates suicide. Her life keeps spinning deeper and deeper into a realm of addiction and self-loathing. One day, she decides to leave it all behind and go back home, where she, once again, runs into her simple-minded friend.

They begin spending a lot of time together, to the point where he proposes to her. She refuses, saying that there is no way that he could love someone like her. Finally, that night, she gives in to passion and sleeps with him. She leaves early the next morning, trying to escape her past and her mistakes.

There is a problem, though. Jenny cannot run from her past anymore. You see, she is pregnant with the simple man's baby. She has also been diagnosed with AIDS. The time for running is over. Finally, at the end of her rope, she lets herself be loved by the simple man and marries him. She becomes Jenny Gump. Indeed, her husband was not a smart man, but he knew what love was.

You see, Forrest Gump had to deal with Jenny's baggage for almost twenty years. He was there for her at all times, even when she pushed him away. He loved her; he was supposed to be there for her. Did that mean that it was easy for him to love her? Of course not. There were hard times, and he kept getting rejected over and over again for more than two decades. That is dedication; that is choice and commitment to love. Think about it: Would you be willing to keep opening your heart to someone who was not trustworthy who would probably break your heart again and again? Forrest Gump had a Christlike love for Jenny. In fact, his story reminds me of the minor prophet Hosea's struggles in his love life.

You may not know much about Hosea. His book in the Bible is nestled snugly behind Daniel (page 687 in my Bible, if you are following along). "When the Lord began to speak through Hosea, the Lord said to him, 'Go, take to yourself an adulterous wife and children of unfaithfulness, because the land is guilty of the vilest adultery in departing from the Lord'" (Hosea 1:2). Hosea is commanded to marry a prostitute. A hooker. A strumpet. By God. The Bible does not divulge much information between the marriage and the first child, but we can only postulate that there were serious issues. A prophet of the Most High God and a prostitute. The original odd couple. This poses some interesting questions. Did he try to tithe her income from prostitution?

But seriously, this is tragic, is it not? Gomer gave Hosea three children (were they even biologically his?) but was always out practicing her trade. Hosea was left to sit at home and wait for her to return from committing adultery. It was a sad, empty life that reflected the way Israel was treating her bridegroom, God.

> The Lord said to me, "Go, show your love to your wife again, though she is loved by another and is an adulteress. Love her as the Lord loves the Israelites, though they turn to other gods and love the sacred raisin cakes." So I bought her for fifteen shekels of silver and about a homer and a lethek of barley. Then I told her, "You are to live with me many days; you must not be a prostitute or be intimate with any man, and I will live with you." (Hosea 3:1-3)

Hosea's love redeemed his adulterous wife. Did all of the problems end there because he took her back? Of course not. He probably dealt with the pain from this for the rest of his life. But he also learned how to love his wife the way she needed to be loved. Hosea offered her unconditional love and was able to meet her where she was even though it cost him dignity and honor among others. His friends were probably telling him to kick her to the curb (or the nearest sand hill) because she was not worth the trouble, but his love was stronger than ridicule or shame.

"Come home, darling, come home quickly. Come home, darling, all is forgiven. So come home quickly."

—"OF MINOR PROPHETS AND THEIR PROSTITUTE WIVES," PEDRO THE LION

You see, the person in the relationship with the baggage carrier is given a unique, difficult trust. Not everyone is strong enough to deal with these issues day in and day out. In fact, no one is really strong enough to handle these problems on their own. It takes the redemptive, supernatural love of God working through you for it to succeed. You have to be a willing vessel. In order for you to decide your worthiness of the task at hand, I have compiled some questions that you need to ask yourself to see if you are willing and/or able to deal with the demons a person may have in their life.

If it is a moral issue, does your partner see anything wrong with what they are doing?

What are they doing on their own to make this better? Are they praying daily for grace and strength? Are they putting themselves in that situation each and every day? It is one thing to pray for strength against lust; it is another to pray not to lust when you go to the strip club. Remember the Israelites assumed that God would go with them wherever they went; they did not take into account the fact that God would not go with them if they were being disobedient. They have to be praying against this stronghold, but also physically be getting up and running away. If Joseph had not run away from the temptation of Potipher's wife, he would have slept with her and probably been put to death by his boss. It takes the same prayer and effort on their part as it does on yours. Faith and action must work together to overcome the baggage.

Are you willing to accept the fact that you will be unable to fix it on your own?

You must remember that not all problems can be fixed in a short period of time. In fact, the ones that I classify as "demons" are those that persist, those that are in our sinful nature (Rom. 7:21). Do you have the patience and humility to accept this? Do you truly realize that someone's behavior is not based upon your actions? Step one of the Al-Anon program (for loved ones of alcoholics) is to admit powerlessness over the loved one's disease. If you try to force it, then you will end up in a codependent relationship that will slowly strangle you. It is impossible not to be concerned, but do not worry. Worry adds nothing to the mix. You can be there as a support, but it is not your goal to fix the situation. It is an exercise in futility.

Are you able to overlook these things in this person?

Some people are not able to do this. Is it narrow-minded? Not necessarily. Personally, I think that anyone whom God has forgiven should be forgiven by me as well. But if the person does not fit your standard for dating, then do not bother. If they have done something that you will resent, then simply do not go out with them anymore. After that, spend some time searching your soul to see if you have forgiven them as well. Just remember that it is possible to forgive somebody but to also cease being with them. If your boyfriend beats you, then you need to forgive him; but you also need to get out of the relationship.

Carrying baggage is tough and difficult; there are long, painful nights that are a definite struggle. You must realize that if you make the choice to commit to this person, you will be expected to cope with these problems. It may not seem fair, but just remember that your partner is learning to cope with your problems as well. When times are tough, just ask yourself: is this person worth it? If you love them and you are committed to them, then you know what you need to do.

Lastly, do not try to play the martyr. If you "put up" with your SigOth's problems so that people will see how good and patient you are, then the problem will persist. The key phrase in Baggage Basics is not, "Woe is me" but rather, "God, help them and heal them." Be strong, and take heart.

Oh yeah, and make sure to encourage the Abigails in your life.

CHAPTER SEVEN

THE LONG-DISTANCE CHALLENGE

Meet Rebecca. She and Josh have been dating for some time now and are each other's first SigOth. She graduated high school with his younger brothers, so she mainly knew of him but did not know him. He accompanied her group on a mission trip and started to develop an attraction toward her.

He began initiating conversations with her, and she freaked out because she had never had anyone pursue her so seriously, especially someone she knew to be the type of guy she would consider dating and/or marrying. All along she never considered dating a guy she didn't think might be someone she would consider marrying if the Lord continued to bring them together.

He began telling her he loved her and talking to her more. This was at the end of the summer before her freshman year of college. She moved away for college in the fall, and they continued talking via instant messenger and email. He never stopped expressing interest in her, and after a while she realized he was serious.

"It's thoughts like this that catch my troubled head when you're away, when I am missing you to death. When you are out there on the road for several weeks of shows and when you scan the radio, I hope this song will guide you home."

— *"SUCH GREAT HEIGHTS," THE POSTAL SERVICE*

Finally at the end of the next February Rebecca told Josh that she loved him, and that is when they decided they were officially "together." Of the four summers she has been in college, two of them have been spent at home near Josh. So their relationship has been long distance from the start. They have spent more time physically apart than together. They are lucky if they see each other once a month, and sometimes it's been even longer than that.

Rebecca's story tells us exactly how difficult long-distance relationships can be. But it also shows that love can endure all things if you are willing to sacrifice and trust God. In fact, as of this writing, Rebecca and Josh are planning their wedding and just bought a house.

The question that begs to be asked is: Why are long-distance relationships so prevalent among young adults and college students?

I think this occurs for a variety of reasons. Some long-distance relationships begin when people who are dating choose to attend different colleges or universities. Or they participate as counselors in summer camps and meet someone from another part of the country and get together. It is easier, thanks to the globalization of technology, to get in touch with someone. You can't see me in person? Try the phone at my house. Did my machine pick up? Call me on my cell. Don't want to leave a voicemail? Just email me or text-message me. Somehow, someway we will get in contact. It is much easier to communicate over vast distances. For that reason, couples are forming over a considerable distance, or already-established relationships have to endure being physically separate from their SigOth. To best understand this concept, we must differentiate between being apart for a short amount of time (i.e. summer) versus a long amount of time (i.e. Rebecca's story).

SHORT-TERM

Whether you are simply going home to spend time with family, going to work at a camp, or going on a mission trip, you may find yourself spending a significant amount of time away from your SigOth. Often, relationships like these falter, but, if acted upon properly, they can lead to you having an even deeper relationship with your SigOth. Alison and I had been dating for three months when it came time for her to go away to work at a camp for the summer. Being separated by a twelve-hour drive brought a new perspective to our relationship. She and I both knew that the summer apart was going to make or break our blossoming relationship. That summer was a learning experience for each of us, and we learned many lessons about how to properly care for each other when we were unable to be physically together.

Time is a commodity.

Alison worked at Camp Mystic that summer, a camp in Hunt, Texas, situated down by the Guadalupe River. The term lengths for her camp were one month, so that was the only time I would get to see her. One time she came to visit me, and another time I went to visit her. Just once a month. The beneficial part of that is that Alison and I were able to treat any moment that we had together as sacred and important. Any time that we would talk, we would always say, "Just think; thirteen more days and we will get to see each other." The very thought of getting to spend time in the presence of my girlfriend kept me going day in and day out. The thought of getting to see her again every day after the summer ended kept me driven while working in my dad's store.

It is really easy to say that the time together is not that important. After all, it takes a lot of money and extra effort to be together like that. But in a long-distance relation-ship, the cost is well worth the reward. If you do not get to spend some time physically together during that time apart, then you are truly making matters worse. You will find an increase in stress and a tendency to be less cordial to each other when you do talk. Have you ever wondered why you fight sometimes when you are apart? You do not necessarily resent your SigOth, but you might resent the fact that you two are apart. It is very frustrating having to be apart, but spending time together can help alleviate your concerns.

Just being in the company of the one you love puts everything into perspective.

Write letters to each other.

You also need to write letters to each other. Not email, but letters. If you do not realize the power in receiving a letter from the person you love, then you obviously have never gotten one. There is so much power in written expressions of love. The main problem that I have with emailing your SigOth is that it is too easy. It takes maybe five minutes to write an email and click "send." Maybe. There is no real cost involved, so less genuine thought is used. Take the time to write letters. Handwrite them even if your handwriting is atrocious. There is more heart in a handwritten letter of love than in a typed letter.

During my time apart from Alison, we would write four to five letters a week to each other. At first I did not see the importance in such an act until she called me a week into camp sad that I had not yet sent her a letter. So for thirty-seven cents I was able to make her day whenever she got a letter. It was the highlight of my day as well when I would receive a letter from her, and I would read it dozens of times each day. I even bought a small box to store every letter in. It is good to have those words of affirmation written down so that you can look back on them whenever you need to. The power of spoken words will eventually fade or be forgotten. Words written down can be kept and read again and again. Trust me, you will still read these letters years later and know how much they love you.

Distance yourself from people of the opposite sex.

I do not mean to avoid them like the plague, but do not spend any quality time with them that might lead to something else or be perceived to be leading somewhere else. Remember you are still committed to your boyfriend or girlfriend. It makes them feel honored to know that even if you are hundreds of miles apart, you still treat the relationship as you would if they were across town.

Think about it. What is the benefit of spending time alone with another OSF while your loved one is away? What is the motivation? Feelings can stir at any moment if you allow yourself to be in a situation that cultivates them. Loneliness can lead people to do stupid things. If you are feeling lonely for your SigOth, write them a letter, call them (if your schedule allows), or talk to God about it. Too much time with an OSF might confuse feelings, especially when your SigOth cannot be there to reassure you. Save yourself the trouble and set yourself apart from the OSFs.

Pray for them daily.

Of course, you should be doing this when you are together as well, but praying for them when they are far away brings you two together on another level. To know that somewhere out there many miles and hours away, your SigOth is also praying for you can connect you in a deep and meaningful way. Set a time each day where the two of you pray at the same time for each other. It is a moment where your souls will touch. Pray that they are still seeking God and not getting caught up in the loneliness of being apart from you. Pray that they are growing from their experience and that the things they learn will be applicable to you as well.

After all, you are appealing to each other through your kindred spirits even though you are hours away. Pretty sweet, eh?

LONG-TERM

Consequently, the rules for long-term, long-distance relationships require a slight change in perspective. Spending each day for the foreseeable future over a considerable distance is not fun, but it is very doable. To succeed in long-term, long-distance relationships, these measures should be taken.

Distance yourself from people of the opposite sex.

This rule is the same as for short-term apartness. Rebecca offers a unique view in how she handles being apart from her SigOth. She never feels tempted to flirt with other guys, but loneliness has been a huge burden she deals with. She has plenty of friends but still yearns to spend time with Josh and see him. Although she never flirts with other guys, she reached the point where she would question whether they were meant to be together because of this intense loneliness. She is a pessimist, so she would think incessantly about their relationship and focus on all the negative things until they were blown out of proportion in her mind to the point that she forgot all the wonderful, positive things about her and Josh. She would question if they should break up because of the blown-up, miniscule negative things, just

"We always speak when you're so far away, and I'm sitting right here. It's 10:00 your time and it's 1:00 by mine."

—"THIS IS NOT A LOVE SONG," THE JULIANA THEORY

because she did not have Josh there physically to remind her of all the wonderful things that attracted her to him. Pessimism combined with distance is not a good thing.

In a long-distance situation, flirting with people of the opposite sex is not a good idea either. If you mix loneliness and a desire to be loved with a flirtatious nature, you will find yourself in situations where you may develop feelings for someone nearby and forget about your long-distance SigOth altogether. If you truly want your relationship to flourish with your SigOth, then you need to remain faithful. Do not let a root of attraction develop for anyone else.

Pray for them daily.

Again, this one is the same as mentioned earlier. Pray for strength, pray for the aforementioned loneliness, and pray that they are not letting distance keep them from loving you or from being effective where they are. I have known people with SigOths a long distance away who would spend all of their time pining for them instead of taking the time to enjoy the people who were with them. I have not seen many relationships thrive in which either person does not establish an identity where they live.

> "Suddenly, we're apart, and I can't see you every night. Though we'd fight, I loved you so much; now I can't feel your touch."
>
> *—"O GIRLFRIEND," WEEZER*

So that is an essential prayer need. Another focus of prayer should be a peace about the relationship. Pray for assurance and a reminder that this is all in God's will.

Another prayer need is for each of you to honor each other and resist temptation when you are together. When Alison and I were able to be together that summer, it was very difficult to not kiss and touch her all the time. My emotions were so strong—strong in my love for her, strong in the fact that we were actually in the same room, and strong by the idea that she was as excited to see me. Thank God for strength because that was the first time in our relationship that I really considered sex with Alison to be a possibility. Thankfully we saved it for marriage, but the temptation was very strong, and it is a serious issue that each of you needs to be praying about.

Use a variety of methods to communicate.

Living far apart limits your means of communication to just a few ways: telephone, email, and instant messaging. Email and instant messaging are so convenient but can also be very impersonal. In this area, I highly recommend telephone conversations. But a word of warning: if you do not have direct-connect minutes, be prepared to spend a lot of money on phone calls. I had a friend in my dorm whose girlfriend lived hundreds of miles away. Since this was before rampant cell phone use, he had to use standard long-distance calls to talk with her. They would talk for hours each night; at fifteen cents a minute, the talking got expensive. In fact, my phone bill would be around $20, and his would easily top $400 each month. He valued talking to her so much, he would never be able to go out for food with us because he kept all of his money for phone charges.

For Rebecca, her conversations with Josh at first were instant messenger and email with a few phone conversations every once in a while. Eventually the means of communication shifted to the telephone. To avoid the "you said you would call and you did not" problems that often arise in long-distance relationships, they set up a time of day that he would call her and a time she would call him. He called her in the morning, and she called him at night. Initially she was longing for much more communication than he gave, so she had to work through her issues by praying and talking to God. Recently, she ordered the same cellular phone service that Josh has so they can make use of unlimited direct-connect minutes.

Coping with the distance was not hard for Rebecca at first. She told people that it was good because it made them talk and get to know each other without the distraction of being together and being sidetracked by the feel-good feelings that come from him being in the same room as her. It forced her to focus on aspects of personality and compatibility.

In addition to phone calls, it would be wise to invest in stamps. For thirty-seven cents and a few thoughtful words, you can make your SigOth's day. On special occasions, care packages are another way to let your SigOth know they are in your thoughts. During my brief time apart from Alison, we would send each other packages once a month in honor of our monthly anniversary (or is it "monthiversary"?). She sent me a ring that said, "Wherever you go, I will follow," and I sent her books and a framed picture of us. These are mementos that each of us still hold onto and cherish to this very day. Of Gary Chapman's five love languages (physical touch, quality time, service, gifts, words of affirmation), only one (physical touch) cannot be utilized over long distances. When you write a letter, you are taking quality time to serve your SigOth by sending them a gift filled with words of affirmation. I cannot overemphasize how critical letters can be to the development of a long-distance relationship. They cannot bring your loved one into the same room, but they can alleviate anxiety and give your heart a moment of respite as you count down the days until you get to see each other again.

Long-distance relationships can be very difficult and frustrating. After all, you want to be able to spend time with the person you love. But you need to remember there is a reason that you two are apart for so long. If you keep focused on God and why you love your SigOth, you will find your bonds growing stronger and stronger. If it is God's will for you to be apart in that time, then it will all have been worth it when you come back together. In situations like that, absence truly makes the heart grow fonder. Think of this time as a unique, awesome opportunity for your relationship to grow.

Oh yeah, and make sure you send them unsolicited presents.

CHAPTER EIGHT

SEX AND THE SINGLE CHRISTIAN

Meet Kevin and Kelly. Kevin and Kelly are leaders in their college Bible study group. Each of them mentors and disciples several people, and they are active in promoting the Gospel. Kevin and Kelly started dating about a year ago. They made a vow with each other to abstain from kissing and beyond until marriage. They spend hours and hours with each other talking about their lives and their future together. One night, the moment hits just right, and Kevin and Kelly kiss. It is one of the most beautiful things that either of them has experienced. As they part ways that night, each of them feels overwhelmed by what just happened.

The next night they talk, but both of them are still think-ing about the kiss from the previous night. Eventually they are kissing again, and this time it turns into a make-out session. The next night the talking is at a minimum and the kissing is heavy. This goes on for several days, and one night during the kissing session, hands start wandering. They agree that it is OK as long as intercourse does not occur. One night soon after, they get drawn into a deep session again and agree that "just this one time" will be OK. After all, they are getting engaged soon. That one time turns into a nightly thing, and the talking all but stops. Kevin and Kelly cannot see that while they are having sex, the rest of their relationship is diminish-ing. Soon, all they have left is the sex, and they are not sure that they even love each other anymore.

"Daughters of Jerusalem, I charge you by the gazelles and by the does of the field: Do not arouse or awaken love until it so desires."

—*SONG OF SOLOMON 2:7*

In society today, sex is ev-erywhere. Sex is selling beer, chips, and even promoting PETA. We live in a sexual world and are sexually driv-en beings. This combination often leads to disaster. The Church is not exempt from sexual problems either. How many times have pastors had to resign because of affairs with secretaries or women within the church? There is a problem here that is not going away anytime soon. If you think you are immune from these difficulties, make sure that you do not fall (1 Cor. 10:12). You are often closer to the precipice than the rest. So much sexual-related be-havior is done in the name of love. Soap opera after soap opera showcases men and women who were tricked into "making love" with someone else, as if the act itself always expresses love. Many great evils in life have been done in the name of love, and it is easy to see how sexual immorality can be justified. We use many statements and questions to tell ourselves that it is OK to give in to the temptation.

How is it adultery if we're not married?

Let us look at one of the Ten Commandments, and see what it says about sex: "You shall not commit adultery" (Exod. 20:14). Adultery occurs when you have a sexual relationship with someone other than your spouse. For instance, when Alison and I were dating, we knew that we were going to get married. However, we both understood that to become sexually involved before we were married would be cheating each other when we did become married. Basically, I did not want to cheat on Alison Taylor (my wife) with Alison Sosebee (my girlfriend). Adultery can be committed even when neither of you is married. Think of it in another way: if you engage in sexual activity before you are married, you are having sex with another man's wife or another woman's husband.

> Do not lust in your heart after her beauty or let her captivate you with her eyes, for the prostitute reduces you to a loaf of bread, and the adulteress preys upon your very life. Can a man scoop fire into his lap without his clothes being burned? Can a man walk on hot coals without his feet being scorched? So is he who sleeps with another man's wife; no one who touches her will go unpunished. (Prov. 6:25-29)

No one will go unpunished. Thank God for grace. This is a serious issue, and we need to realize that sexual behavior has real–life consequences. Pregnancy, STDs, and broken hearts are left in the wake of undisciplined sexual behavior.

It is our responsibility as brothers and sisters in Christ to encourage and build up each other. If you sleep with your girlfriend, you are not only dishonoring her, but you are also dishonoring another man's wife and another man's daughter. Proverbs 5:20 says, "Why embrace the bosom of another man's wife?"

How far is too far?

Is kissing too far? How about heavy petting? "How far is too far?" is the question asked by many Christians these days. What is the motivation behind the question? What does it even mean? The problem is that asking that question is akin to asking, "How close can I get to sin without it being sin?" We want so badly to identify with the experiences and pleasures of the world that we keep trying to push the line again and again. Each time we make a compromise in this area, the line gets pushed a little further back. My old university minister John Strappazon said that our physical attractions are like a car without brakes. All you have is an accelerator. Once you get started, it is next to impossible to slow down. Alison and I had our first kiss (my first kiss ever) approximately one month into our dating relationship.

After that, talking just did not seem as important. After all, what is the fun in talking when you could be kissing? It took a lot of discipline, but eventually we were able to establish communication even after the kiss. It was difficult, but it was worth it in the long run.

But back to the problem at hand. If your desire in your dating relationship is to simply not "sin," then neither you nor your partner will ever reach the heights of greatness and righteousness for which your relationship is designed. In the movie *Office Space,* Peter is discussing with the consultants the problems with motivation in his workplace. "[Not getting hounded by my bosses] is my motivation for working—that and the fear of losing my job. But you know, Bob, that only motivates me to work hard enough not to get fired." Working not to get fired and acting not to sin are dangerous. Greatness is not achieved by avoiding failure. Avoiding sin only leads to a lukewarm, mediocre relationship that is destined for failure and sadness.

"But among you there must not be even a hint of sexual immorality."

—EPHESIANS 5:3

Texas Tech recently implemented a program belonging to the Gallup Organization called StrengthsQuest. According to the program, we need to build up our strengths instead of fixing our weaknesses. Weakness-fixing leads to well-roundedness. "Well, that does not sound so bad," you might say. True, but the problem with well-roundedness is that it leaves no room for a person to have an edge; just a group of individuals who are all semi-good at everything. Play to your strengths and work to improve the relationship with positive ideas. Treb Praytor once said that the best way to remove the air out of a glass is to pour water into it. If you try to remove the air without filling it with something else, then the glass breaks. We are creatures designed to be filled. Do not merely avoid crossing the line. Stay as far from the line as possible.

We may not have said our vows in front of others or in a church, but we said them to each other and before God. And that's good enough for me.

It is a joke, and we all know it. I spoke with a friend, who gave me this as her justification of engaging in premarital

sex. She is willing to say anything in the world to justify
it and make her feel right about violating statutes that she
probably once held. Ladies, let me give you some advice: If a
guy is pressuring you into doing things that you do not feel
comfortable doing, then he is not acting in love toward you.
He is looking to satisfy his own needs, not yours. In marriage, the husband's body becomes the wife's and vice versa.
If you are not in a committed married relationship, then
you always have the option to leave; after all, your body still
belongs to you. What is one of the reasons for the marriage
ceremony? Is it just to show off and fall into the norm? No,
it is so that you can be held accountable to the vows you
made in front of everyone.

My brother stood on the steps at First Baptist Church in
Lubbock, Texas, and saw me take my vows to Alison. He
knows that I have made a commitment, and if I ever start to
stray from it, I expect him or anyone else who was there to
tell me. You make those vows in front of others in order to
be held accountable to the commitment you make. It is like
a profession of faith in Jesus; if you only do it in private, then
you will have no one to help you in the tough times—you
can just walk away. You need a witness to sign off on your
marriage license to make it legit, so that you do not just decide one day that you are married. Marriage is not a spur-of-
the-moment decision; it is a life-changing decision that needs
to be treated with the utmost respect. Making vows to each
other is a sacred and solemn thing and should not be used as
an after-the-fact excuse in an attempt to justify the behavior.

If you are dating somebody or engaged and you know for a
fact that you will marry the person you are with, then you
owe it to them and yourself to wait until you are married to
have sex. God designed sex for a husband and wife, not for a

boyfriend and girlfriend who "just know" that they are going to get married.

Your virginity is not a prize to present to someone else; it's yours to manage in your own best interest.

According to this point of view, you do not owe your future spouse anything. "It's yours to manage in your own best interest" really means "give it up if you think it will help you." It takes love totally out of the equation. Ladies and gentlemen, I implore you that your virginity is a prize that is to be presented to your husband or wife on your wedding night. It's a way to tell your spouse, "I waited for you, and now your body is mine and mine is yours." Your best interest is not merely what feels right at the moment. Long-term thinking must be used when it comes to decisions about sexual behavior.

You see, the problem is that sex has come to mean so many different things than what the original intention was. Sex is a means of procreation, but it is also a way for a husband and a wife to show their love for each other. It has been corrupted and changed into a selfish means of fulfilling our needs. We go into sexual relationships looking for our pleasure alone, and wonder where the meaningful sexual expression has gone. Here is a hint. It is in the marriage bed. Meaningful, healthy sexual relations occur when two individuals are totally committed to each other, make their vows public, and are looking to please their spouse. That is the sexual relationship that God honors, because it honors Him.

I'm sure there's more than one Mr. Right out there, but you have to familiarize yourself with the crop in order to sort the proverbial wheat from the proverbial sleazebags.

This is an actual quote from an actual website that dispenses relationship advice. Apparently, getting to know someone has shifted away from communication and common interests to sex. Sex, it would appear, is the primary factor in determining the effectiveness of a relationship. Interesting. But it's totally wrong as well. The combination of two personalities and love for each other is the number one sign of an effective relationship. If a guy is a jerk to you in conversation, he will be a jerk to you in bed. If a woman is rude, she will be rude in bed. Entering a relationship is not like shopping at Wal-Mart. You cannot just return someone else's heart or their sexual expression and receive a full refund. Every time it costs you a piece of yourself. If you keep giving yourself away, one day you will be left with nothing but a shell of bitterness and shame.

> "'Everything is permissible for me'—but not everything is beneficial. 'Everything is permissible for me'—but I will not be mastered by anything."
>
> *—1 CORINTHIANS 6:12*

As you can see, many people deceive themselves with what they perceive to be healthy sexual behavior. It is no wonder that the Christian culture has conflicting ideas and confusion about the proper expressions of sex. I remember in junior high when my Sunday school teacher told the class that when two people have sex, demons pass in between them. Although I feel he said this to scare us from doing it, it shows that the Church likes to rely on a culture of fear and shame with regard to sex. Sex makes people feel very uncomfortable. After all, Adam and Eve both hid themselves when they realized their nakedness. And most believers have hidden in shame and guilt about their sexual nature in the name of decency and modesty.

While everyone is hiding, today's twentysomethings look around and wonder what exactly they should do. What are the standards of proper, godly behavior? When is it OK to have your first kiss?

Meet Katie. She went out with a guy to her high school homecoming event. It was her first time to be asked out since junior high. She and her guy were in the back of a horse-drawn carriage ride going through downtown, a perfect romantic setting. During the ride, he leaned over for a kiss, and she just started coughing in his face and all of a sudden "became ill." She made up a horrible excuse about being sick and totally ruined the moment. He knew she was just nervous and avoiding him. So at the end of the night, he decided he was not giving up and asked for a kiss on the cheek (a harmless thank you for a wonderful evening, he said). When she went in to kiss him on the cheek, he quickly turned his head, and she ended up kissing him smack on the lips. He said that was his way of easing her out of being so nervous about a kiss. In my opinion, he is lucky that she did not punch him in the face.

When to kiss for the first time is open to much speculation and debate. I have known couples who have refrained from kissing until their wedding day, while others have kissed on their first date. As I said already, Alison and I waited about a month to kiss. Is there really a right or wrong answer? As with many theological issues, the proper boundaries have more to do with a person's motivations and intentions than their actual actions. Kissing, therefore, is not too far unless it leads to sexual arousal in you or your partner. A kiss is probably not a good idea if it leads directly to intercourse or making out.

Meet Matt. Matt is a big fan of the Nintendo 64 game *PilotWings*. It is one of the first games he played on that system, and he loves it; specifically, he loves the music for it. On one level (the birdman stage) if the player gets close to the ocean, he hears really relaxing music. So one night he and his girlfriend are in his room, and he has a great idea. He turns off the lights and turns on the game. He picks the stage and flies himself next to the water, so they can hear the waves and the nice relaxing music. They lie down on his bed and just stare at the ceiling while a man in a bird suit stands next to a virtual ocean. Then he realizes exactly what he is doing. She is freaked out, and he feels like a nerd. They do not even make out. Matt won the birdman level that night, but he lost cool points with his girlfriend.

Is it necessarily bad that they did not make out? I cannot say. But you and your SigOth need to utilize the self-discipline and accountability that characterizes a healthy relationship in order to overcome the temptation. One good plan of action is to respect each other's torsos. Any physical contact below the neck or above the knees is too personal for a dating couple. This area of the body is designed for arousal when touched by the person whom you love.

In each of the surveys, I asked an open-ended question to the volunteers: "What is one thing you will not compromise in a dating relationship?" Ten guys and twenty-two girls specifically mentioned physical boundaries or standards for sexual behavior. How interesting that more than twice as many girls than guys said sex. Although I do not feel it reveals anything profound (girls are just as sexual as guys), it is something to ponder. Several others said that beliefs would not be compromised, which can also be loosely interpreted as sexual behavior.

Why is that? Why on earth did I make that connection? Why do any of us? Have our beliefs in relationships become so tied to the physical act of sexual intercourse that we ignore every other boundary? I do not know. But I do know that there are many unhealthy decisions that can be made that are as bad as (if not worse than) intercourse.

But hopefully, this chapter has given you some insight into the dynamics of this integral aspect of relationships. Maintain discipline, stay focused, and treat each other with respect.

Oh yeah, and don't spend time alone together after midnight.

CHAPTER NINE

CHIVALRY OR CHAUVINISM?

Meet Kim. Kim has been dating a guy for a few weeks; he loves music, he's funny, cute, and rugged. The only problem is that he is also weird. One night, they go to a movie. He is three to four paces ahead of her as they head into the theater. In the lobby, he once again turns it into a foot race. The problems grow as a malfunction with the lights in the theater keeps the movie from starting. His decision? He tells Kim to go tell someone to take care of it while he continues munching on popcorn. For some odd reason, she went out with him again. According to her, she wanted to give the guy the benefit of the doubt. He takes her out to dinner. At Taco Bell. They once again go to the movies, where he nudges her to buy her own ticket. Ouch. Inside, he once again puts on his running shoes and walks ahead of her. He becomes so unaware of her existence that when she stops to chat with a friend, he is halfway through the line waiting to buy another bucket of popcorn. Suffice it to say, Kim never went out with him again.

> "Why do you sing Hallelujah if it means nothing to you? Why do you sing with me at all?"
> — "DELICATE," DAMIEN RICE

Kim's plight is quickly becoming a typical one for people these days. In the twenty-first century, ideas of gender roles are hot topics that leave many people confused. How do biblical ideas of spiritual leadership fit into the equalization of societal expectations? Who is responsible for what in a dating relationship? Questions like these plague individuals before the relationship even begins.

Should the guy always ask the girl out?

In each of the surveys, the question, "Should the guy always ask the girl out?" was posed to the volunteers. In The Real Man Survey, 46 percent of the guys said that the guy should always ask the girl out, and 48 percent said no (6 percent said it depends). I was not really concerned with the answer as much as I was with the reasoning behind the answer. When pressed for why they feel the guy should not always ask the girl out, guys offered up some of the following reasons (see Appendix B for a full list):

"No. If a girl wants to ask a guy out, then she should. But because of how it's been in the past and 'sexual politics,' it seems like that rarely happens."

"Women like feeling empowered and (at least a little) in control of every aspect of their lives, so I think not sticking to the old viewpoints is a good way for equality to come in during any potential relationship."

"No, some guys are too shy or too stupid to realize that a girl likes him."

In the "no" responses, I saw two prevalent themes: they either brought up the "outdated ideas" of the guy having the burden to ask the girl out or they used the "guys are dumb" card. In all honesty, I feel that the "guys are dumb" card is one of the biggest cop-outs that the vast majority of guys practice. The statement generally goes like this: "Girls try to drop all of these hints, but I am just too dumb to figure it out. If she would just come out and tell me that she liked me, it would be way easier because I am too slow to pick up on things like that."

While in some cases guys might take a little longer to pick up on hints, they still need to step up, take the lead, and be men. Girls, on the whole, would say that guys are just as confusing as girls when it comes to mixed signals. No girl is going to show you totally how she feels unless you share part of your heart as well. Therefore, she has to use signals.

And here are some reasons why guys said they should always ask the girl out:

"If the girl is the first to show interest, then she should not be afraid to ask a guy on a date. Although, if the guy knows that she is interested and he has a mutual interest, it is only proper for him to take the initiative and ask the girl out."

"Yes, God has called the man to be a leader in a relationship, and if he can't even initiate a date, then he will never be able to initiate leadership in a relationship."

"From what I understand, girls like to be pursued. That doesn't mean she can't drop hints, though."

The guys that said "yes" brought in ideas of spiritual leadership and the need to initiate the relationship from the beginning. Before I comment further, let's see what the results from The Actual Female Survey looked like. Of the fifty ladies, 68 percent said that the guy should ask the girl out every time, while 32 percent said no.

Here is what the ladies who said "no" had to say:

"Guys shouldn't have to always be the ones to put their hearts on the line."

"No. Some guys are a little too shy or do not think that you think that way of them. Sometimes a girl has got to take the reins and do it herself."

"In our society it tends to be a taboo for a girl to take on this role. What is the deal here? Are guys afraid that women are too dominating or worse, desperate, just because they ask out a guy? It takes a man 1.9 light-years to get the hint. Sometimes we women grow old and die before they get around to asking us out, so we just have to go and·do it ourselves."

These ladies, it would seem, are tired of the guys not asking them out and have decided to "take the reins" and "go and do it [themselves]." In their eyes, guys are not doing their jobs, and they are growing tired of it. It seems that deep down even those who say "no" would really prefer to be asked out but seem resigned to the fact that they will have to step up and start doing the asking. The ladies who said that the guy should always ask the girl out have the same attitude, but just from a different perspective.

"If the guy is worth his salt, he will have the gumption to ask a girl out. It proves that he is confident, self-motivated, and able to stand on his own two feet."

"I think sometimes as women we want a leader in the guy. We chase the guy and strip him of his leadership role. We then marry the guy and are upset when he is not leading! Also I think when a guy is interested, typically he will show interest. Guys go for things more it seems, and when they want something they go after ... it's good to let the guy do the 'chasing.' Then we, as women aren't left wondering ... Does he like me? I think if he likes me, he's going to show it!"

"Relationships always work better if the guy is motivated to be in it. Lots of guys will just say 'yes' to a girl who asks him out because they think, 'Well, why not?' Or they don't want to hurt her feelings, but their level of commitment is probably way less than hers. It's better to wait until it's the guy's idea because then he'll stay in it."

"It is always way more fun to have the guy ask the girl out, because then she really feels like she is worth it."

These ladies really want to be asked out because it shows the guy is taking the chance for her. I had a friend say one time, "Girls feel pretty when guys ask them out." Guys, the girl really wants to be pursued. She wants to see you make the effort to be with her. Recently we had a really hard snow out on the South Plains. The worst day of the weather was when Alison, Clark, and I had to drive to see my family for Christmas. On the drive, we passed through the Llano Estacado, which is essentially an arid region with a lot of dirt and oil wells. But in the snow it was one of the most breathtaking sights I have seen. The advantage of living in a flat area is that you can see miles and miles of snow-blanketed land. I was in awe. The roads were very dangerous, however; ice was thick on the road. It occurred to me that if I had not risked driving on ice, then I would have never encountered the beauty of the snow-covered Llano. Experiencing beauty involves risk. Guys, it is very risky to ask a lady out. But if she says "yes," then it is the most beautiful thing possible; how exciting it is to have an attractive girl interested in you. Take the risk. It is well worth it.

Those who spoke of the "guy asks girl out" ideal either saw it as an out-of-date idea (from the negative perspective) or just as being old-fashioned, almost apologetically (from a positive perspective). But just because an idea is old does not mean that it is irrelevant to modern times. The idea of chivalry was discussed by a few respondents. Chivalry, in the sense of being polite and putting others first, is a sign of maturing spiritual leadership and is something of which guys need to be conscientious.

The other day I was watching the entrance to the Texas Tech library, observing patterns in behavior. For the hour I watched, only three guys held the door for someone else. There is something seriously wrong when a simple little thing like holding a door becomes forgotten by the guys. Well, guys, let me offer you a bit of advice: It might be a little thing to you, but to the special girl for whom you hold the door (or don't hold it, as the case may be), it means everything. As one respondent put it, *"Cheers to men who still know what chivalry is and don't wimp out with the 'things are different in this day and age' crap."*

I have a friend who shared an interesting story with me about a guy not acting chivalrously. In college, she went on a blind date with this guy who had recently graduated from the university. He picked her up in a nice sports car (of which he was very proud), and when they got in the car, he wanted her to listen to some CD he had just bought. Keep in mind, they had never previously met, so it is expected that conversation would take place. Well, imagine trying to "get to know someone" who was trying to talk over this ridiculously loud heavy-metal music. The music was blaring so loud that they could see each other's mouths moving, but there was no way to hear anything that the other said. There was a lot of smiling, nodding, and pretending to follow the conversation. She

> "I want a girl who will laugh for no one else. When I'm away she puts her makeup on the shelf. When I'm away she never leaves the house. I want a girl who laughs for no one else."
>
> *—"NO ONE ELSE," WEEZER*

had such a huge headache by the time they got to dinner that it did not even bother her that the entire dinner conversation was centered around tracks 6 and 8 on the album. This guy obviously forgot the most important part of the dating experience: making her feel special. Do not worry just yet about discussing the spiritual meaning behind Stavesacre's latest album; get to know each other, and have a good time.

It is safe to say that women have an innate desire for guys

to act like men. The guy should act like the leader from the get-go. The leader? Wait. What does that even mean? Well, let's take a look.

A PROBLEM VERSE?

I am about to present one of the most misquoted, misunderstood, misused verses to which people like to refer. It is a verse that "socially conscious" people look at and judge the whole Bible on. They read it out of context and use it to justify their discrediting of the Bible. It is also a verse that bigots and chauvinists look at and interpret the rest of the Bible with. They read it out of context and use it to justify their misogyny and their out-of-date ideals. The verse?

"Wives, submit to your husbands as to the Lord." (Eph. 5:22)

Two types of people misread that verse; actually, they only read the first part of it and ignore the last part. Today's feminist subculture does not like any hint that a man has authority over a woman. They do not bother to understand the historical context or even the context of this verse; they read this and see the Bible as an outdated, male-dominated book.

Of course, there are also the narrow-minded men who read that and think, "Dang right! I have authority over the woman, so she needs to do everything that I say." This verse does not allow for domestic slavery of any kind. There are four magic words there that have been overlooked: "as to the Lord." What does that mean exactly? Does that mean that they put man on the same level as God and thus both of them dominate the woman? Of course not.

Ephesians 5:25 says, "Husbands, love your wives, just as Christ also loved the church and gave himself up for her." Marriage is a picture of Christ and the Church. Since dating is a precursor to marriage, it is safe to say that the man has some semblance of leadership in the dating relationship as well. For the sake of the discussion at hand (leadership in dating), we will look at the picture of the marital relationship in the context of dating (although some differences apply, as you will see).

If a man is not acting in a Christlike way toward his girlfriend, then he is violating the task with which God has entrusted him. A girlfriend is supposed to submit to a man whose motivations and intentions are in line with the attitude of Christ. If a man is not acting like Christ and trying to use sinful behaviors as a way to dominate her, then she need not submit to him because he is not submitting to God. Ladies, if the man you are dating or planning on marrying is not willing to submit to God or to lay down his life for you, then he will not be able to lead you spiritually. In fact, he will not be able to help you or encourage you to any type of growth. If a man is not growing in God when he is single, it is foolishness to think he will grow when he is in a relationship (as with anything, though there are a few exceptions). Take a realistic view of the situation. It is very likely that an unteachable boyfriend will one day be an unteachable husband and father.

I think it is important to realize the passage that begins with this "controversial verse" ends with, "However, each one of you also must love his wife as he loves himself, and the wife must respect her husband" (Eph. 5:33). Now, that is not so bad, is it?

What do you mean by "leader"?

People have several problems with the idea of a man being the spiritual leader of a woman. They derive several connotations from the term "leader." They feel that the term "leader" means that the person who is leading is better than the "followers," has more power, and has authority over the followers to impose his will upon theirs. This could not be further from the truth. A leader is not someone who is better than his followers; he is someone who brings out the best in those he leads. In fact, I am going to throw the term "followers" out the window. The proper term for the girl's role in the relationship is not "follower" but "challenger." Ladies, you are not asked to blindly follow your husband in anything that he does. If he is not submitting to God, he is not leading you in a way that you deserve.

> "Husbands, love your wives, just as Christ loved the church and gave himself up for her."
> —*EPHESIANS 5:25*

But, Jeff, why do I need to be led anyway?

In truth, you should not need to be led. Being led by your husband does not mean that you are spiritually dependent upon him. Each of you should be able to feed off each other and grow. But if you find yourself unable to grow at all without your partner's help, then you are depending on them too much for your spiritual growth; you are, in essence, a spiritual parasite. To make a long story short, you should be able to grow on your own. But once you get married, the game changes. You have two individuals trying to live together and trying to grow spiritually while encouraging each other to do the same.

In *What's the Difference*, John Piper discusses a very effective rule about being a spiritual leader. He says that the man, as the leader, has the final say in any and all situations (unless he is acting sinfully) but will and should often give up what he wants in situations where sin is not present so that his wife can have her preference. This may not sound fair, guys, but it is all about making her happy and making her feel important. To be a man is not to use your supposed authority to dominate—it is to sacrifice of yourself so that your family can have just a little more. Christ leads us through service and sacrifice, and we men need to do the same.

THE WOMAN'S ROLE

Ladies, I am here to tell you that submission does not equal weakness or servitude. In fact, I am going to tell you that one of your primary roles as a girlfriend, and ultimately as a wife, is to challenge your boyfriend, and husband, to keep growing. You need to push him to greater things and not let him accept mediocrity. But some guys do not like it when women act like that. They feel as if the woman is being too dominant. For some reason, many guys are afraid of being challenged by a woman. Why is this? I can think of a few reasons.

Chauvinism

A lot of guys have this unconscious thought that men are superior to women, and any woman who poses any sort of challenge must not be dateable because they do not know how to "submit." Of course, in this case, guys have a strained view of what ideals like "leadership" and "submission" mean, as we have already discussed.

Intimidation

This goes along with chauvinism, but it is slightly different. Ladies who are confident and willing to challenge guys are attractive, but they can also be very intimidating. Guys are constantly struggling with whether or not their strength is sufficient in every aspect of their lives. To be challenged by a woman means that it is possible for the guy to fail. Guys do not like to fail, so many of them opt out of that type of relationship so they will not let anyone down. This is faulty thinking as well because it eliminates a guy's strength and causes him to accept mediocrity.

Laziness

Guys tend to get lazy when it comes to relationships. For us, the thrill is in the hunt, and as soon as the prize (i.e. the relationship with the woman) is won, we tend to slack off and slow things down. A challenging woman will not accept that, and some guys avoid them because it just takes too much effort to work on the relationship. Why do you think you see more women than men in marital therapy? Why have more girls asked me questions about their relationships than guys? Guys put the work in trying to get the girl, while ignoring and/or neglecting what makes her happy when in the relationship.

My advice? Stay away from the guys who do not wish to be challenged. They are not ready to be disciples, and they are definitely not ready to love you the way that God intended.

So now that we have clarified a few issues with regard to spiritual leadership, I want to address leadership, specifically in a committed dating relationship. You see, in marriage the boundaries are very clear about leadership. But in a dating relationship, what are the rules? What does a developing leadership role look like? I can think of a few dos and don'ts.

DO encourage her to grow in her walk with Christ.

It will help you grow as well to see the woman that you love giving her life over to God. A relationship built on encouragement can only grow and deepen. You come to realize that her spiritual state is as important (if not more) to you as your own. When you see areas of growth, tell her. Be specific. Let her know that you are amazed by how much she has grown.

DO hold her accountable.

This one can be tricky because the more you get to know someone, the more you come to recognize sin patterns in their life. The key words here are gentleness and respect. If you come right out and tell her that she has a problem with gossiping, she is likely to get defensive and not listen to what you have to say. Trust me. When she feels she can trust you with her negative traits, she will confide in you the problems that she is experiencing. Even then, she is not looking for a coach, just someone to lovingly support her while she attempts to grow. Of course, this dynamic can go too far.

DON'T attempt to disciple her.

Discipleship is one of the keys of the Christian life. It has no place, however, in the dating relationship. Being the spiritual leader does not mean you are her total resource for support; she needs godly women for that. When you mix strong emotions with discipleship, emotional and spiritual promiscuity ensues. What happens if you break up? Where will she go for help if you have been her sole source for support and guidance? Back off and let her grow spiritually through other people as well.

DON'T pray together while you are alone.

This one sounds odd, but many problems can result from this. One problem that could occur is the weakening of defenses to sexual temptation. If you are by yourself with the person you love and you are taking part in the most intimate spiritual act, what is to keep you from someday moving to the physical? That sounds very absurd, and part of me does not want to write it down, but it is true. When I have serious prayer time with a person (not just blessing a meal), I need to hug them when I am done. I feel very close to them. Mix in strong emotions and a strong attraction, and it could be a recipe for disaster. That is why I recommend waiting for this until you are married as well. It is another level of intimacy that we tend to cross with the first person who shows interest in us. Remember that the enemy will try to use the best times of our life for ill. He is not above trying to use your prayer time as a battle for sexual purity. That is why it is best to refrain from it until marriage.

Gender roles in this day and age can be very confusing. But I feel that the Bible still offers the most relevant ideals about what each person's role should be. The man is the leader; the woman is the challenger. If you feel as if you are not doing your part, just pray about it and then start trying to do it.

Oh yeah, and offer to buy her some popcorn, too.

CHAPTER TEN

CONCLUSION

Meet Adam. Adam and I have known each other for many years now. He was in my wedding and has been an excellent friend. Adam also has a penchant for getting into awkward situations with the ladies.

One such time, he was at the mall looking for a new backpack in Eddie Bauer.

Enter cute girl, to his left. He spends a few moments debating whether to establish contact, but no good lines are coming to mind. And he has to have a good line. Otherwise, he'll walk up, trying his best to be cool, and end up spouting out something about how all his friends think he is just like Seth Cohen from *The O.C.*

Suddenly, he becomes aware of a single unsettling fact that means his chances with this girl are now quite low.

He has just walked into the side of a Coke machine.

Coke's been getting pretty fancy with its machines lately. The newer ones have an elevator/conveyor belt thingy. Very high-end stuff. But apparently, for this particular model, Coca-Cola took some cues from the Romulans to design the coke-machine-of-prey, a Coke machine with cloaking technology.

> "Good luck exploring the infinite abyss!"
> —GARDEN STATE

Anyway, he sure didn't see it, but he sure did walk right into it.

I can just imagine what this girl might have told her friends. "This really creepy guy at the mall was checking me out, and I thought he was going to talk to me. Luckily he got laid out by a Coke machine."

Adam's story is not unique. Thoughts of love and attraction can have a profound (and sometimes debilitating) effect on anyone's life, as I have shown you. You have read many clever ideas about how to handle relationships. But right now, they are just ideas. They worked for me because I actually applied them in my life. These pretty words will do nothing for you unless acted upon.

Either make a point to apply your clever ideas or throw them out the window. Ideas are only good when they are put to use. An intangible idea can often be used as an excuse for not acting the way you feel you should in a relationship. In other words, head knowledge means absolutely nothing unless it is applied in your life, intentionally.

Intentional is an adjective that is rarely used or deserved these days to describe others. Too often we meander about aimlessly, allowing ourselves to be tossed by the winds of change and wondering where things went wrong.

It all comes down to a difference between humility and shame. Are you worried that others might be unimpressed with who you are? Are they out of your league (in your eyes)? Are you worried about how to put up a good front and sell your positive qualities in order to get a date?

> "Try not.
> Do or do not.
> There is no try."
>
> *— STAR WARS:*
> *THE EMPIRE*
> *STRIKES BACK*

Let me ask you a question. Have you ever had a job interview? I am going to give you the key to a successful job interview. If you can perfect this one trick, then your chances at getting a job (even above more qualified applicants) goes up. If you can turn the interview around on the interviewer, then it is in your hands. If you find yourself asking more questions and taking an interest in the interviewer, then the job is all but yours. Why is that? You are showing an interest in the person you want to work for and the position that is open. Interest in the position shows a strong desire to be there, and asking questions of the interviewer opens him or her up to you and creates a bond. Do not be overzealous in trying to promote yourself; worry about showing the interviewer an interest and how you would fit in with the company.

Do you see what this has to do with talking to girls yet?

C.S. Lewis, in *Mere Christianity*, said this of a humble person: "Probably all you will think about [the humble man] is that he seemed a cheerful, intelligent chap who took a real interest in what you said to him." Open up the floor; let them talk about themselves. You see, everyone loves talking about themselves when someone shows interest. If someone keeps asking me questions, it says to me that they are interested in what I have to say, that my ideas and views are valuable.

> "In wisdom gathered over time I have found that every experience is a form of exploration."
>
> *—ANSEL ADAMS*

It all comes down to your intentions in a relationship. Are you looking to be loved? Or are you looking to invest in someone else? Hopefully, the answer is both. It takes a lot of work to do it. But we are adults who can learn new things. Do not let harmful or lazy patterns prevent you from the relationship that God wants you to have. Do not beat yourself up about the past; just let God's grace strengthen you to try harder next time (Titus 2:11-12).

Make a point to show your love. Go the extra mile. You may feel that it's most unromantic to make a list of things to do for the one you love, but that could not be further from the truth. You have to choose day by day to love the person you are with and to find ways to express your love.

Love is very special; it is designed by God to give us happiness, to get a glimpse of heaven on earth. Feelings can be very confusing and weird, but when looked upon in the light of God's truth, they can enable us to love the way we are designed. Watch out for those friendlationships. Share your feelings, live life, and take risks.

Oh yeah, and watch out for those Coke machines.

THE ACTUAL FEMALE SURVEY

The Actual Female Survey was conducted between August 16, 2004, and November 8, 2004. It was conducted over the Internet through email correspondence. The answers were offered by a group of fifty females ranging in age from adolescence to middle age. The participants volunteered via email after a request was offered for volunteers from *www.jefftaylorministries.org*. All participants' names are confidential, and the responses and opinions offered in the answers are the opinions of the participants and are not necessarily the opinion of the author. This is an informal survey and should not be treated as statistically valid.

1) AGE:
<20 — 16% (8)
20-24 — 60% (30)
25-29 — 14% (7)
>29 — 10% (5)

2) WHERE ARE YOU FROM?
Texas — 68% (34)
California — 12% (6)
Delaware — 4% (2)

2% each (1)
New Mexico
Alabama
Illinois
North Carolina
Connecticut
Missouri
Minnesota
Ontario, Canada

3) WHAT IS YOUR CURRENT RELATIONSHIP STATUS?
Not dating, but I have my eye on someone — 24% (12)
Not dating, and not looking for now — 22% (11)
Married — 16% (8)
In a serious relationship — 14% (7)
Engaged — 10% (5)
Not dating but looking (write-in) — 8% (4)
Might be dating someone — 6% (3)

4) WHAT IS THE MINIMUM AMOUNT OF EDUCATION YOU EXPECT FROM YOUR IDEAL GUY?

Bachelor's degree — 56% (28)

Some college — 20% (10)

High school diploma/GED — 10% (5)

Doesn't matter — 10% (5)

Master's degree — 4% (2)

Doctoral degree — 0% (0)

5) HOW DO YOU WANT YOUR GUY'S INTELLIGENCE TO COMPARE WITH YOURS?

As smart as you — 72% (36)

Smarter than you — 28% (14)

Not as smart as you — 0% (0)

6) HOW DO YOU WANT YOUR GUY'S AGE TO COMPARE WITH YOURS?

Older (less than five years) — 56% (28)

Same age — 34% (17)

Younger (less than five years) — 4% (2)

No answer given — 4% (2)

Way older (more than five years) — 2% (1)

Way younger (more than five years) — 0% (0)

7) WHAT TYPE OF GUY WOULD YOU PREFER?

Athletic — 50% (25)

Artistic — 44% (22)

No answer given — 6% (3)

8) HOW OFTEN WOULD THE IDEAL GUY WORK OUT?

Twice a week — 44% (22)
Every other day — 36% (18)
Once a week — 10% (5)
Every day — 2% (1)
Once a month — 2% (1)
Don't care (write-in) — 2% (1)
As often as he wants (write-in) — 2% (1)
No answer given — 2% (1)

9) WOULD YOU RATHER YOUR GUY HAVE A:

High E.Q. (emotional quotient) — 50% (25)
High I.Q. (intelligence quotient)- 42% (21)
No answer given — 6% (3)
Both (write-in) — 2% (1)

10) WHAT IS THE TOP QUALITY YOU LOOK FOR IN A GUY?

Godliness — 60% (30)
Sense of humor — 28% (14)
Honesty — 10% (5)
Intelligence — 2% (1)

11) WHAT IS THE ONE QUALITY YOU AVOID IN A GUY NO MATTER WHAT?

Dishonesty — 58% (29)
Arrogance — 26% (13)
Emotional instability — 10% (5)
Lack of confidence — 6% (3)

12) A NICE GUY ASKS YOU OUT, BUT YOU DO NOT FEEL ATTRACTED TO HIM. WOULD YOU ...

Say, "No, not at this time." — 52% (26)
Say, "Yes." — 22% (11)
Say, "Maybe sometime in the future." — 16% (8)
Say, "No, never." — 12% (6)

13) IF YOU WERE DATING A GUY AND REALIZED YOU DID NOT WANT TO MARRY HIM, WOULD YOU ...

Break up right away. — 52% (26)
Wait for the right time to end it. — 44% (22)
Give yourself time to "come around." — 2% (1)
Do nothing. — 2% (1)

14) YOU LIKE A GUY. HE ASKS YOU OUT, BUT DOES NOT HAVE ENOUGH MONEY TO BUY YOUR DINNER. WHAT DO YOU DO?

Find something to do that is free. — 72% (36)
Say yes and pay for your own. — 14% (7)
Say yes, but expect him to find a way to pay. — 6% (3)
Say yes, and pay for both meals. — 6% (3)
Say no. If he did not have the money, he should have never asked you out. — 2% (1)

15) DEFINE "DATE."

Two people go somewhere, one pays, they're attracted to one another.

Anything a guy and a girl (who are interested in each other) do together by themselves, or in a group if their attention is mainly focused on each other, to get to know one another a little better. A date could be as simple as taking a walk, or it could be as stereo-typical as going to dinner and a movie.

A meeting arranged in advance where a guy and a girl spend time together.

Plans made prior to the event that include only the two of you spending recreational time together.

A date involves a guy asking a girl if he can hang out with her with the intention of getting to know her in a way that is deeper than just a friendship. A date can involve a meal, a movie, a game, etc. There is no defined "date," just the date itself.

A guy and a girl going out or hanging out with a romantic intent.

A time for two people to talk and learn about each other. This is done with just the two of them around. It's a time when you learn what the other person values and believes and determine if you feel that you like what they stand for.

Two people of the opposite sex enjoying each other's company to-gether while trying to get to know each other and determine if they should continue in the relationship.

A date is an activity of sorts, initiated by the guy to be able to spend time with the girl, while hopefully having a nice time and discovering if there is any romantic interest between the two.

Spending time together, outside of the everyday routine time. A designated place, outside of the home typically.

When a guy requests the company of a girl to go to dinner, movie, concert, etc. There are clearly romantic interests on either side or at least a strong desire to get to know the person more. There should be no confusion as to what the guy or girl's intentions are when going on a date.

Spending time with someone.

An outing that can be during the day or at night in which the individual who asked for the date sets up, plans, and pays for an activity or a meal as a tool to get to know the other person whom the individual asked out.

Doing something with someone of another gender with the understanding that there's mutual interest.

A time period where two people spend time together getting to know each other better and have a good time. Although some dates are anything but, that is the ideal to most people at the beginning.

When two people who think they like each other as more than friends hang out with one another in order to get to know each other better.

Going out with someone that you like and can have fun with and be yourself. It doesn't have to be expensive to be fun.

When the guy asks the girl out, and they do some activity specifically in an effort to see if they are interested in pursuing a dating relationship (dating just each other).

A "date," I think, would be the traditional situation in which a guy and a girl go out alone or in a group—but does not necessarily imply "romance" or the possibility of a future relationship.

Two people doing something together with the goal of determining if they are meant for each other.

When both parties agree and are aware they are participating in activity as more than friends. The guy is responsible for making his intentions known.

A date is an emotionally casual outing for the purpose of getting to know a member of the opposite sex better. Dating more than one person at a time is acceptable.

An opportunity to go out with someone whom you have interest in; chance to learn more about someone and have fun together (hopefully).

A date is planned time spent one-on-one. That's all. It could be coffee, dinner, dancing, etc., or it could be driving around together looking at houses, or it could be walking to the grocery store to get cookie ingredients and then baking cookies. Planned time. One-on-one. Those are the keys—unless you put "group" in front of "date," and then I guess anything goes.

Two people going somewhere with the mutual understanding that you want to pursue the idea of being more than just friends. Spending time getting to know one another, with no physical displays of affection (i.e. kissing).

A guy and a girl doing something together, one-on-one, that is fun for both and allows them to get to know each other better.

The guy picks up the girl, takes her out—and if it costs money, pays for it—and takes her home. This doesn't pertain to a dating relationship.

A date is a nice casual get-together at an eating establishment or a bar in an effort to learn more about another person.

When a guy asks a girl to go eat dinner, movie (somewhere neutral) to talk, and get to know one another. There might have been a previous friendship or just interested in personality or looks.

Getting to know someone of the opposite sex that you could potentially marry.

Going to do something together, just the two of you, with intentions of finding if a mutual attraction could lead somewhere.

Two people of the opposite sex who enjoy each other's company spending quality time together to get to know each other better.

In my opinion, a date is when one person asks the other to go out/hang out exclusively. This could include dinner, a movie, lunch, or mini-golf, whatever.

If you are already dating, it is an experience that you do together that deepens your understanding and appreciation of the other person. If it is a first date, it is an experience for the purpose of illuminating the other person's character so you can better know if they are a possible marriage partner or not.

When a girl and a guy are spending prearranged time alone together for the purpose of getting to know each other for a possible romantic future.

A guy and a girl spend time together alone or in a group with the purpose of getting to know each other more intimately on either guy or girl's account. He pays, unless it's free.

An appointment to spend time with someone you love.

I think a variety of types of activities qualify. Food is generally a good call. My fiancé and I like to spend time reading the Bible or other devotional books together. We carry a picnic blanket in the back of the car, so we are always prepared whenever a park or other lawn presents itself. But I definitely have enjoyed the opportunity to get dressed up and go to a nice restaurant too. Obviously, you can't do this every weekend.

Getting together in an agreed-upon location to talk and get to know each other as potential marriage partners; may or may not include food.

A guy and girl go out in public to a restaurant or some type of entertainment activity.

A date is time spent together, whether alone or in a group, that allows you the opportunity to see another side or aspect of the person you're interested in. A date can consist of many things, such as just coffee, dinner and a movie, cooking for the person, etc. ... activities that allow you to get to know that person better and see how they react in various situations.

Male and female going somewhere together to get to know each other better.

A "date" is any time spent together when:

> *a) It is just the two of you, and no one has defined it as a "just friends" outing (note, if there hasn't been any sort of definition, most girls would consider alone-time with a guy a date).*

b) It is with a group of people, but one of the two specifically asked the other without clarifying that they are "just friends" (though there are also exceptions to this—if it is a friend you regularly spend time with, and the invitation is more of a casual "oh by the way, the gang is doing this on Saturday ... you coming?" sort of thing—that isn't necessarily a date).

That's hard to define. But I would normally say when a guy and girl go out, and the guy pays. And he treats you like a lady while you're out, not just a friend. I can tell the difference in a guy buddy paying for me just because and a guy that is interested. I get treated better with the date.

Spending time, getting to know a person, and sharing something fun ... movies, arcade, park, animals, etc.

A date is when two people agree to spend time together to learn more about each other, with a possibility of a future relationship.

Spending quality time with one other person. No distractions just one-on-one.

A guy asks you out, picks you up, and pays, and you both like each other. Friends can do this same thing, and it does not qualify as a date.

Spending time with a person you're interested in getting to know.

A girl and guy with feelings for each other hanging out to pursue something more than friends.

Going out on the town with someone of the opposite sex with the intentions of pursuing something more (group or individual).

A meeting arranged in advance where a guy and a girl spend time together.

16) SHOULD THE GUY ALWAYS ASK THE GIRL OUT? EXPLAIN.

He should probably be the one to ask for the first date because I don't think it's really a girl's responsibility to get the ball rolling—guys should be brave enough and leaders enough to ask and start things off. After that, I don't have a problem with girls doing the same—we're a pretty modern society.

I think it is nice when the guy takes the dominant role to ask the girl out, but I don't think that it is completely out of the question for the girl to ask the guy out. It is a very scary thing to open up and tell someone how you feel about them. Guys shouldn't have to always be the ones to put their hearts on the line.

Yes, I feel like it is just a part of their gender role to do so.

For the first few dates the guy should always ask the girl out. I believe this because I believe that it is not the girl's role to pursue a guy. We are supposed to wait for the guy to "declare his intentions" as I have heard it said before. Once two people are "dating," I feel a girl is not stepping out of her role in asking the guy out.

Most of the time, the guy should ask the girl out. Sometimes, though, the girl may have an event through her work, school, etc. that she needs to ask someone to go to with her.

No, I think the girl can ask the guy out. Sometimes guys are too shy, and if the girl sees something in the guy, she should go for it.

Yes, because most Christian girls want a guy who will be able to be a spiritual leader for them in the future. By demonstrating leader-ship skills at the beginning of the relationship, the girl is getting to see the guy act this out and the guy is getting to practice the whole leader thing.

Absolutely. If the guy is worth his salt, he will have the gumption to ask a girl out. It proves that he is confident, self-motivated, and able to stand on his own two feet.

Yes, in my opinion the guy is the leader at all times, and that should certainly be from the get-go. It should not be the girl pursu-ing the boy more aggressively.

I'm quite traditional when it comes to "dating." I believe it is the guy's job to do the asking out. I want to date/marry a guy who is confident and is a natural leader. If a guy is afraid to ask you out, I would take that to mean he lacks the confidence to go out on a limb and take a risk.

Not necessarily. Some guys just don't figure things out fast enough.

Not necessarily. It is more appropriate for the guy to ask the girl out and take her to dinner, a movie, or an activity for which he pays, etc. But it is appropriate also for the girl to ask a guy if he would like to come to her apartment or house for dinner (she makes dinner) or ask if he would like to go to a casual activity, like an outdoor concert. Normally, however, I think that the guy should ask the girl out.

Yes. He should ask.

No. Some guys are a little too shy or do not think that you think of them that way Sometimes a girl has got to take the reins and do it herself.

That's a tough one, because if a girl doesn't just come right out and express interest, the guy may never know that she likes him. So I think that girls need to learn to take more chances.

It just seems more proper for the guy to ask, but nowadays girls ask as much as guys do.

Yes, I feel this is the way God created it, for the man to pursue the girl. I think sometimes as women we want a leader in the guy. We chase the guy and strip him of his leadership role. We then marry the guy and are upset when he is not leading! Also I think when a guy is interested, typically he will show interest. Guys go for things more it seems, and when they want something, they go after it ... it's good to let the guy do the "chasing." Then we as women aren't left wondering ... Does he like me? I think if he likes me, he's going to show it!

I don't think that a guy should ALWAYS ask a girl out—I think it is cool if a girl asks a guy out—but in our society it tends to be a taboo for a girl to take on this role. What is the deal here? Are guys afraid that women are too dominating or worse, desperate, just because they ask out a guy? It takes a man 1.9 light-years to get the hint.

Sometimes we women grow old and die before they get around to asking us out, so we just have to go and do it ourselves.

Yes. If he wants me to follow later on, then he better lead from the beginning.

I believe the guy should ask the girl out because he is the leader of the relationship. This sets the pace for the entire relationship.

Yes. Relationships always work better if the guy is motivated to be in it. Lots of guys will just say yes to a girl who asks him out because they think, well why not? Or don't want to hurt her feelings, but their level of commitment is probably way less than hers. It's better to wait until it's the guy's idea because then he'll stay in it.

No, I think girls are fully capable of asking a guy out. This girl, however, would never have the guts to do it.

While I feel that it might set a better precedent for the relationship if the guy is more of the instigator (he is the one who would eventually end up asking for the hand in marriage and taking the responsibility as the head of the relationship), I think that a girl shouldn't be afraid to let the guy know how she would feel about being asked out.

Yes. Girls are more likely to put an emotional connection to the outcome and be affected negatively by rejection. Plus the man is supposed to be the leader of the relationship, and that needs to start from the very beginning of the relationship.

Not necessarily. Some guys, just like some girls, may just not have the confidence to even think that a girl may like him, so he takes no initiative in pursuit. Or a girl may be fed up with the guy beating around the bush, and she just may want to find out where they stand. This being said, it is always WAY MORE fun to have the guy ask the girl out, because then she really feels like she is worth it.

The guy should always ask the girl out. It is biblical. If the girl does the initiating, then what is left for the guy to do? Christ pursues the church, not the other way around.

No. Sometimes guys are intimidated asking a female out. I, myself, am a prime example. Most guys say that they feel that since I look mean, that I am mean. After they get to know me, they like me because of the personality I have.

No, not always. If a girl really likes a guy, she should ask him. There should be no waiting on either part.

Not necessarily, but I think that it's wise to let the man lead in his role. I never asked my husband out, but just gave him subtle hints that I would like to get to know him better.

Yes, I am a traditional girl. I think that the guy should always initiate, after that it is fair game.

Yes. Women want leaders. We want guys who will take the initiative because when we do find the guy we are going to marry, that guy is supposed to lead.

No, I do not think the guy should always be the one to ask out. Sometimes there are guys who just never ask girls out. If a girl knows this, then she should feel comfortable to ask him out if she wants. I would PREFER a guy to ask me out, and I never have asked a guy out. Also, I think that sometimes the girl needs to hint at the guy, like "you should call me, and we should hang out," etc. Then it makes the guy know the girl wouldn't mind him asking at least that. It's good for the girl to hint. But I also do not think it is bad for a girl to ask a guy out. Everyone's situation is different, and I do not think defining "rules of dating" could ever or should ever be followed.

Yes, because the man is called to be the leader.

I just want to be pursued. I feel like Christ pursued us as a church, when He gave Himself up for us … so I want to be pursued by a guy because the picture of marriage between a man and a woman is supposed to be like that of Christ and the church.

Yes. It shows his ability to take initiative and be a leader, which is important, even in that stage of the relationship.

Yes. I believe it is the man's place and calling to be the initiator, and the pursuer. Once the relationship is firmly established, I think there is a little more room for the woman to pursue him, to call him, suggest dinner, etc.

Yes. I want (and have) a man who's proactive and initiates!

Yes, because I believe it's the guy's job because that is how it was way back then.

I still believe in a lot of the old-fashioned rules for dating. For instance, I like having my door opened, I want my dad to be asked permission for my hand in marriage, and I like to be treated like a lady. However, I am not opposed to "helping a guy out" if he is nervous about asking me out and yet I know he wants to. I will make it as easy as possible for him to know that I would not reject him if he were to ask, or I'd even suggest going out for coffee some-time to further break the ice for him.

I am not going to ask a guy out, but not everyone feels the same way. But I most certainly want the guy to ask me out. It shows courage, and that he is willing to take a risk for something he wants.

Yes. We're all chicken. Girls AND guys. Read Wild at Heart *by John Eldredge. Especially the part where he writes about the man as wanting to be the rescuer and the woman who wants to be pursued and rescued. Enough of this silly gender confusion. Males and females are EQUAL, but still DIFFERENT and still with different roles to play. Cheers to men who still know what chivalry is and don't wimp out with the "things are different in this day and age" crap.*

Every time I've ever been interested in a guy and let him know, it's done nothing for me, so I stopped being the initiator. Maybe I'll never have another date because guys are too wussy to ask girls out, but I guess I'm old fashioned or something or I just got sick of being turned down.

I believe so. A man should want to be around me enough to ask.

The guy should be the pursuer. It's not the girl's place to be directing the relationship.

YES! If a man is supposed to be the head of the household and spiritual leader in a relationship, he better have the confidence early on to be assertive and take the initiative. Plus women today are expected to be so strong and independent, but then we lose the ability to learn how to submit to our husbands as they do to us.

Yes. I think that a girl asking a guy out continually puts her in the leadership position, whether that is acknowledged or not.

No, definitely not. I asked my current boyfriend out, and I'm glad I did. I don't play by old-fashioned rules. I think either person should go for what they want.

I would say no because sometimes guys don't get the hint that a girl likes them. However, I, like most girls, don't like to ask guys out.

No, not always. Although, I prefer it for myself, I do not believe that all girls are clear about their intentions. Guys are usually just as worried about rejection as girls are. In a perfect world, guys and girls would feel comfortable and secure enough to be honest about their feelings to one another.

17) WHAT IS ONE THING YOU WILL NOT COMPROMISE IN A DATING RELATIONSHIP?

If it's clear that it isn't God's will, we should end the relationship immediately—otherwise, it's just a big waste of time.

I would never compromise my morals or beliefs in a dating relationship. I have very strong beliefs, and while I might be open to a small difference in his views, I would never go back on something that I personally believe in just to keep the relationship going.

I would never compromise sexual purity. It is definitely not morally right to have sex before marriage. That is very important to me.

Christian beliefs.

The one thing I will never compromise in a dating relationship is where I stand on my belief of and my relationship with the Lord.

Values and what I want in a partner.

My feelings on sex.

My religious beliefs and the religious beliefs I look for in a guy because I have tried relationships in the past in which the guy did not share my beliefs and, in some cases, even wanted me to change them, and I have found through personal experience that those relationships don't work out so well.

One thing? Geez. I have to pick ONE?? I absolutely refuse to date a guy who cannot tolerate my family, or even if he does not enjoy them.

I am my family, just as crazy, so he needs to love them.

A guy that speaks "ugly" to me in any way, a guy that "puts me down" joking or not, or a guy that "loses his temper."

Sexual purity is one thing I will not compromise. For me it is a very important thing that should and will only take place within the confines of a marriage. Honesty is also very important to me. A lack of communication or not voicing cares and concerns will cause problems. Having a completely open and honest relationship is the only way, in my mind, to have a healthy and strong relationship.

Sex.

Self-worth for someone else's arrogance or need to make themselves feel smarter by making me feel less so.

I'll only date someone who's a Christian.

My beliefs (religion, morals, etc.).

Morals.

Your belief in Christ and all that He expects out of us as Christians. A guy is not worth it nor is a girl. If they like you or even love you, they should understand your feelings or they are not worth having to begin with.

Spirituality.

I have experienced this before: I will NEVER compromise my own integrity in a relationship. I will not put up with a relationship in which I am not wholly and completed respected (including both my physical self and my mind—my ideas and beliefs) and nurtured. A relationship is a two-way process and should be considered a constant delving-in: you must make a commitment to constantly search and learn about the other person. Without respect, nurturing, and an honor of integrity, this cannot happen, and you are simply wasting your time.

I'm thinking about this one. One thing for certain is my purity. But there are more things than that. Your question got me thinking.

Physical interaction.

I absolutely will not lead on or flirt with a guy just for the attention. I will do my utmost to be honest and sincere because I do not want to hurt or mislead a brother in Christ and possibly someone else's husband.

Sex.

Having made this mistake in the past, and as cliché as it sounds, I would never again compromise the whole "unequally yoked" thing. Lots of times girls make the excuse of "well, he MIGHT be a Christian, we just haven't really talked about all that yet. I don't want to make things AWKWARD after all." Anytime a girl or guy says this, you might as well go ahead and assume that either this person they are dating is NOT a Christian at all, or that if they are, they are certainly not enjoying a shared level of spiritual growth. There is just no way that two Christians, who are actually experiencing a growing relationship with the Lord, will spend any large amount of time together and have the subject just never come up. All that happens when you put that "talk" off is that you become more and more emotionally involved, and then when it becomes painfully obvious that you do not share the same morals, values, or belief system, you have a lot of explaining to do as to why you were ever involved in the first place when it could never really go anywhere.

The amount of physical intimacy that is and is not appropriate in the relationship.

Anything having to do with my faith in God.

My decision to stay sexually pure.

Honesty and loyalty.

My Christianity and beliefs about it.

Sexual purity.

I have not dated in a very long time. I don't know what the circumstances could be. I won't kiss on the first date. I hope to not divulge too much private information. I want to be a woman of God.

My religious beliefs and values.

Dating a non-Christian.

My walk with God. If a dating relationship doesn't push me closer to God, it must end.

Physical boundaries.

Sexual purity.

My sexual purity (saving myself for my future husband).

Going too far.

Sexual purity.

Having sex before marriage.

My relationship with Christ.

My faith and who I am as a person. If I can't be me, I can't be with you. The most important aspect of who I am is my God. Try to take that away or diminish His importance in my life, and you aren't allowing me to be who I am.

My purity.

Sex before marriage/dishonesty.

I will not compromise my physical boundaries.

Sex. Although I no longer have a dating relationship, when I did I guess the biggest thing that was just an absolute NO was having sex with my boyfriend. Any guy I dated had to know ahead of time and be alright with that. But then again I would never have dated a guy that didn't have that same belief as I did.

As a Christian, the typical answer is Christian. So assuming that this is the top answer, I would have to say being respected.

Dishonesty.

My beliefs. Whether it be my religious beliefs, my beliefs about what I want to do or things like that.

THE REAL MAN SURVEY

The Real Man Survey was conducted between August 16, 2004, and November 18, 2004. It was conducted over the Internet through email correspondence. The answers were offered by a group of fifty males ranging in age from adolescence to middle age. The participants volunteered via email after a request was offered for volunteers from *www.jefftaylorministries.org*. All participants' names are confidential, and the responses and opinions offered in the answers are the opinions of the participants and are not necessarily the opinion of the author. This is an informal survey and should not be treated as statistically valid.

1) AGE:
<20 — 14% (7)
20-24 — 56% (28)
25-29 — 18% (9)
>29 — 12% (6)

2) WHERE ARE YOU FROM?
Texas — 78% (39)
Ontario, Canada — 6% (3)
Florida — 4% (2)

2% (1) each
Oklahoma
Missouri
Kentucky
Massachusetts
New Jersey
Arizona

3) WHAT IS YOUR CURRENT RELATIONSHIP STATUS?
Not dating, and not looking for now — 26% (13)
In a serious relationship — 24% (12)
Not dating, but I have my eye on someone — 22% (11)
Married — 14% (7)
Might be dating someone — 8% (4)
Engaged — 4% (2)
No response — 2% (1)

4) WHAT IS THE MINIMUM AMOUNT OF EDUCATION YOU EXPECT FROM YOUR IDEAL LADY?
Bachelor's degree — 42% (21)

Some college — 22% (11)
Doesn't matter — 22% (11)
High school diploma/GED — 6% (3)
Master's degree — 4% (2)
Doctoral degree — 2% (1)
No response — 2% (1)

5) HOW DO YOU WANT YOUR LADY'S INTELLIGENCE TO COMPARE WITH YOURS?

As smart as you — 78% (39)
Smarter than you — 14% (7)
Not as smart as you — 6% (3)
No response — 2% (1)

6) HOW DO YOU WANT YOUR LADY'S AGE TO COMPARE WITH YOURS?

Same age — 50% (25)
Younger (less than five years) — 34% (17)
Older (less than five years) — 6% (3)
Way younger (more than five years) — 4% (2)
Does not matter (write-in) — 4% (2)
Way older (more than five years) — 0% (0)

7) WHAT TYPE OF LADY WOULD YOU PREFER?

Athletic — 52% (26)
Artistic — 44% (22)
Both — 2% (1)
No response — 2% (1)

8) HOW OFTEN WOULD THE IDEAL LADY WORK OUT?

Twice a week — 46% (23)
Every other day — 26% (13)
Once a month — 8% (4)
Every day — 8% (4)
Once a week — 6% (3)
Don't care (write-in) — 4% (2)
No response — 2% (1)

9) WOULD YOU RATHER YOUR LADY HAVE A:

High E.Q. (emotional quotient) — 66% (33)
High I.Q. (intelligence quotient) — 30% (15)
Both — 2% (1)
No response — 2% (1)

10) WHAT IS THE TOP QUALITY YOU LOOK FOR IN A LADY?

Godliness — 70% (35)
Sense of humor — 12% (6)
Intelligence — 8% (4)
Beauty — 6% (3)
All (write-in) — 2% (1)
No response — 2% (1)

11) WHAT IS THE ONE QUALITY YOU AVOID IN A LADY NO MATTER WHAT?

Dishonesty — 46% (23)
Emotional instability — 24% (12)
Arrogance — 14% (7)

Meanness — 10% (5)
All (write-in) — 4% (2)
No response — 2% (1)

12) A NICE LADY HAS A THING FOR YOU, BUT YOU DO NOT FEEL ATTRACTED TO HER. WOULD YOU ...

Sit down and have a talk with her about the feelings. — 48% (24)
Avoid her like the plague. — 26% (13)
Tell her flat out, "I do not have feelings for you." — 16% (8)
Ask her out. What is there to lose? — 4% (2)
It depends. — 4% (2)
No response. — 2% (1)

13) IF YOU WERE DATING A LADY AND YOU REALIZED YOU DID NOT WANT TO MARRY HER, WOULD YOU ...

Wait for the right time to end it. — 46% (23)
Break up right away. — 36% (18)
Give yourself time to "come around." — 10% (5)
Do nothing. — 4% (2)
No response. — 4% (2)

14) WOULD YOU ASK A LADY OUT IF YOU DID NOT HAVE ENOUGH MONEY TO PAY FOR HER?

Yes, but I would find something fun to do that is free. — 72% (36)
No. If I cannot pay for her, then I'd rather not go out. — 24% (12)
Yes, but I would ask her to pay for her own. — 2% (1)
No response. —2% (1)
Yes, but I would ask her to pay for all of it. — 0% (0)

15) DEFINE "DATE."

Two people spending alone-time together talking about more intimate things than the weather. Sharing personal things like their walk with God or past relationships are date-esque conversations. Funny thing is, guys and girls do this all the time but don't call it a date, which in some way makes it OK for them to get their emotions going with no promise of commitment. My girlfriend calls it "shoplifting alone-time."

A date is an opportunity to make an emotional connection with a person. This would be the next step beyond friendship, perhaps leading to a romantic, emotional, and physical relationship.

A meeting between a man and a women who are both interested or committed to developing a romantic relationship and have agreed to spend time together doing something as a way to get to know each other more.

A date is when the guy would intentionally ask the girl out to spend some time to get to know one another. Whether it's eating at a restaurant, going to a coffee shop, or just going to a park or somewhere to talk, it needs to be a time when you get to know the other person. A movie and such would be fine further into the relationship, but is not good to do on a regular basis.

A guy and girl go out somewhere with a romantic setting.

Time spent with someone you want to get to know better.

Something two people do together.

When two people go out that are mutually attracted.

Hmm, a date is spending one-on-one time with someone to get to know them better.

When two people go out.

Two people spending one-on-one time together doing something enjoyable.

When a guy and a girl decide to do something apart from their friends, just the two of them.

Two people with romantic intentions spending time with one another.

date: Previously agreed upon get-together between two people (of the opposite sex) with the UNDERSTOOD intention to set the stage for a possible romantic relationship.

An understood official time with just you and her, that you pay for.

A time that is spent one-on-one with someone that you are attracted to.

The period between just meeting someone and getting serious with them. It's the opportunity to see how well the two of you communicate and determine if there is a future for you.

Going out with someone from the opposite sex that I might possibly have feelings for and have a nice dinner and get to know the person a little better.

Alone with a girl, time to know one another better.

An agreement between two parties to engage in an outing with the intention of beginning a relationship.

The time two people spend with each other due to the fact that there is a mutual interest in either a "romantic" relationship or a potential "romantic" relationship.

When two like-minded people decide to enjoy each other's company.

I know there are such things as group dates, but for the sake of this, I'm gonna stick to two people. Two people spending time together in a scenario where the purpose of the event is to get to know one another better or simply to spend time together in a pursuit of something more than friends. That answer should exclude people going places just to hang out, or going places simply because they want to go. For instance a girl may go on a "date" with a guy to a football game. Here the guy would define it as just hanging out as he most likely wants to go simply to see the game and have someone to hang out with at the time. The girl, however, might see it as a date and an opportunity to spend quality time together. So … is it actually a date if only one person thinks it is? … PUH-TAY-TOE / PUH-TAH-TOE

Date means you have an appointment with a lady going out to have a good time.

A date is when you ask a girl that you're interested in to go do something with you.

Two people spending QUALITY time together doing something they both enjoy. They don't necessarily have to be involved in a serious relationship.

When a man and woman go out to any social function for the purpose of enjoying each other's company and getting to know each other better.

Two adults spending "quality time" alone together

A date is an event the two agree to take part in to get to know each other better.

A date is when a man and a woman mutually agree to go out and either have dinner, watch a movie, play a game, attend a sporting event, or some other form of entertainment where the person who asked, either the man or the woman, pays for the other.

To me a date is when two people go out and they BOTH mutually care about each other in a more-than-friends kinda way. If a guy asks a girl out as more than a friend but the girl doesn't feel the same, then no matter what the guy says to me, that's not a date. I've never ever been on a date, and a great majority of my friends are girls (that I did not and won't pursue to be more than friends).

An arranged meeting between a guy and girl which has been differentiated from a "hang out" time. By differentiated, I mean a time that both parties know has been arranged because there are some feelings of attraction involved.

Two people with romantic interest in each other who hang out in order to get to know each other better.

A date? Two people going out in some sort of social fashion in order to learn more about each other and spend time together. As in dating someone? Two people that enjoy each other's company and exclusivity for the purpose of knowing each other better.

A man treating a woman to some sort of event in an effort to spend time together and show his appreciation for her with the open possibility of both parties being attracted to each other.

Two people of opposite gender go somewhere and do something together for the purpose of getting to know each other better. Romance is indeed a possibility.

Having relationship with someone in order to see if the relationship will lead to marriage. I suck at this stuff.

Going somewhere with someone with the intent of learning about the possibilities for a romantic relationship.

A guy and a girl who are in a romantic relationship doing something which sole purpose is to get to know or be with the other person.

Two people spending time together.

A date is a guy and a girl who are attracted to each other going out in order to better search out their feelings; with the goal of ultimately determining whether or not they are meant to be life partners.

A date is when a guy asks a girl out specifically to spend time with her to get to know her better and then pays for whatever is done that particular day/evening.

Two people with an understood liking for each other meeting at a designated place for the purpose of getting to know one another better or strengthening the relationship.

A prearranged social event involving two people who have some interest in each other.

Going out with a girl and spending an extended time (more than three hours) together with no cell phone, distractions, etc. ... time to focus on each other.

Date: When a guy and a girl do something together that lets everybody else know that they are exclusively going to see only that other person and that they are boyfriend and girlfriend.

Being alone, both open to the possibility of romance, i.e. not being "just friends."

When two people spend time together with the intent of getting to know each other better because of romantic interest.

Two people interested in marriage, and in the hope of getting to know each other to decide whether they have found the person to marry, spend time together in order to discover more about the other.

"A date" is a time spent with another. "To date" is to exclusively court one another for the purpose of exploring whether you are compatible for marriage.

16) SHOULD THE GUY ALWAYS ASK THE GIRL OUT? EXPLAIN.

Yes. It's the guy's role to initiate, and it's the girl's role to respond. If she doesn't wait for his initiation, she is not following him, which, to me, is an indicator that she may not follow him later in life.

No, a woman can desire the same emotional connectivity to a man and is equally capable of pursuing the same.

No. If the girl feels led to approach a guy, she should feel comfortable doing so.

A guy should always take the initiative. He is supposed to be the leader in the relationship further down the road, and for the girl to ask the guy out would be to start out on the wrong foot. Taking into consideration the fact that there are guys out there who have no clue as to whom he should ask out (I am such a person). If the girl is interested in the guy, she could be helpful as to dropping hints saying that she is interested. This does open up the girl to get hurt if he rejects her, but at this point, it's better to be rejected early than to have her invest in him quite a bit, only to find out that he's not interested in her. If the guy does reject the girl early on, it also allows for a friendship to develop in most circumstances.

Yes, I'm old fashioned.

No. Because the girl might be hot and want to go out with you, but if you think it should be "guy ask out only," you'll be sorry.

It doesn't matter as long as you're both happy.

Yeah sure, girls come on to you, but they don't ask very often, and the good ones never ask, cuz they don't have to.

It depends. If the girl is the first to show interest, then she should not be afraid to ask a guy on a date. Although, if the guy knows that she is interested and he has a mutual interest, it is only proper for him to take the initiative and ask the girl out.

Most of the time yes, but if the girl has something she wants to do, it's fine for her to ask.

Yes, it just seems like the man should be in charge.

No, girls should not be shy about asking guys out. If a girl is putting out the "I want to go out on a date with you" vibe, most of the time guys don't pick up on it and vice versa. There is the same amount at risk when a guy asks a girl.

No.

Not always because so many "old-time" stereotypes are going by the wayside these days. And from my experiences, women like feeling empowered and (at least a little) in control of every aspect of their life, so I think not sticking to the old viewpoints is a good way for equality to come in during any potential relationship.

Yes, I guess I am just old fashioned.

No, some guys are too shy or too stupid to realize that a girl likes him.

No, everybody should take the risk in asking someone out.

It really depends on the personality of the person and their experience in relationships.

Yes, because guys are supposed to be the head of the household in a family, thus guys should also be the ones who take the initiative to start such relationship.

Yes. In this day and age, women are becoming a more dominant force, while men are becoming more feminized. It is in these small things that men have to "take back" their manhood and do the deed of asking a girl out. It all comes down to chivalry.

Not necessarily. I don't think it matters who asks who out.

This is outdated and dependent on the traditional definition of dating. Dating is nothing like how it's depicted in the movies, so I don't see why we should act like it is.

In my opinion, yes. The guy should be the pursuer in the relation-ship. The girl can suggest going to hang out if the guy is a little thick headed, but even then the guy at this point should step it up and start to take charge.

Always.

Yes, if the guy is going to lead, he needs to start by initiating the dating process.

YES, God has called the man to be a leader in a relationship, and if he can't even initiate a date, then he will never be able to initiate leadership in a relationship.

I feel it's OK for the girl to ask the guy sometimes. A guy may be interested in a girl but not sure if she feels the same and may not ask because of it. They may not get together at all if she is inter-ested and does not ask him out.

Not always. If the guy likes her, he should ask her out, but if the girl likes the guy, and he doesn't know it, she should ask him out.

In the beginning yes, but once the relationship gets going, it's OK for the girl to suggest things too.

No, a girl can ask a guy out. I see no problem with that, as long as she does not expect the guy to pay. The person who asks is the person who pays.

No. If a girl wants to ask a guy out, then she should. But because of how it's been in the past and "sexual politics," it seems like that rarely happens.

No. The guy should ask the girl most of the time, but there are instances in which girls should ask guys out. Guys can be clueless sometimes and may need a kick start. Although this should be rare.

Yes. Always. The burden of initiative lies on his shoulders. It's the guy's role as leader in relationships.

No way. A girl might see a relationship that would work out easier than a guy might see it. Great relationships might not happen if the girl never asks the guy that didn't see the possibilities.

Unless the girl really wants to take the guy out for a special reason (his birthday, thanking him for something), then yes. I'm a big fan of guys stepping up to the plate with initiation; it's a risk that makes a girl feel special. But a girl could definitely drop hints to let the guy know she's interested and available. Some of us are just plain pansies.

Short answer—yes. Guys should step up and take the initiative. From what I understand, girls like to be pursued. That doesn't mean she can't drop hints, though. Not every guy is on the same level of "courage."

I prefer it. Me personally, I think it's nice, and gentlemanly, and a lot of girls appreciate it, I know I would (if I were a girl, assuming the guy doing the asking out was a nice guy, and not a jerk). With that in mind, I wouldn't have a problem with a girl asking me out. I would appreciate it as well.

Nope. No reason he should.

Yes. I think the guy should sort of "know" if the girl likes him first … then once he does, he should approach the girl.

No. Circumstances are not always cookie-cutter traditional. Who cares who asks who first?

I am pretty old fashioned when it comes to dating, so I believe that a guy should take the girl out for the most part, especially during the beginning of the relationship. I think it is OK for the girl to pay for her own if she wants to after the relationship has progressed a little, but I would feel bad if she paid for me.

Yes, it's the guy's chance to buff up and show that chivalry is NOT dead.

Ideally the guy should be the leader in the relationship, though it can possibly work the other way.

No, girls should step up and ask a guy out if they like them. Most of the time, a guy has no idea what a girl thinks about him until she tells him.

Yep, 99 percent of the time. But there can be hints that the guy can pick up from the girl prior to the first date. After the first date it is completely in the guy's hands to lead the rest of the relationship.

No, because sometimes the guy can like the girl but never have enough guts to ask her out, but the girl does, so then she should be able to take the initiative to hint at it to the guy, but then eventually the guy should, like for the second and so on dates.

No, I think it is fine for a girl to ask.

No, I don't mind getting asked out. But the woman should not always have to take the initiative either.

No, it doesn't matter. Personally, I believe by the point of asking a person out, you ought to know them well enough to be comfortable with her asking. It's not some kind of insult.

No. My wife asks me out periodically, and it is part of the give and take of a relationship.

17) WHAT IS ONE THING YOU WILL NOT COMPROMISE IN A DATING RELATIONSHIP?

My walk with God, and my purity. I've already compromised both in previous relationships, but I absolutely won't do it again. I think I learned my lesson.

Dishonesty and lack of commitment. A friendship requires risk, dating requires the ultimate risk because one lays a friendship on the line in an effort to date. If my dating partner is not equally committed to the relationship, I cannot and will not compromise my emotional status.

I will not, under any circumstances, date a woman who is not a Christian.

Having messed up in dating quite a bit already, I have decided that I will not compromise on time alone. There are times and places to be alone and get to know each other on a personal basis, but there is a lot of temptation that tends to follow. Places allowing you to be alone with your significant other, but are possibly areas to do more than just talk, need to be avoided.

I always drive.

My music and my hobbies.

My style.

If she has had sex a lot. Will not pursue at all.

I will not compromise in spending time with my family. I am a big family person, and every chance I get to spend with them I will, no matter what.

My personality (who I am).

My Christian beliefs.

Faithfulness.

Sex before marriage.

Arrogance and someone who is two-faced—will say one thing and do another—or girls who judge someone for what they do, like, or think.

How I really feel!

My religious beliefs, most definitely!

My identity in Christ.

My religious convictions.

Who I am. I have been in relationships in which I have tried to fit someone's expectations rather than just be who I am. Those kind of relationships never last for long.

Core beliefs. When a person acts outside of what they think is right, the relationship is shot.

What a question, Jeff. For my situation (dating in a college town, and now dating in two separate towns), integrity is extremely important. Here's a fun little scenario/story for you: The other weekend Mandy was coming to town, and by just mentioning that she was coming made people assume that she would be spending the night at my house. Then, the next day at work people assumed I should be in a good mood because they knew I got to see Mandy. Now, I was in a good mood because I saw her, but not because of what they assumed. Not to mention that because we have been dating so long, most people are surprised to hear that we don't live together. Frankly, I'm surprised that they assume we are. I guess that shows the difference in cultures. All that to say that integrity is so hard to gain, especially around people who don't know you. If that means saying goodnight when I don't want to, then that's what it takes.

Never share your woman with another man.

The girl needs to be a Christian.

My faith in the Lord. What I believe to be true in Scripture.

I do not dance, drink, smoke, do drugs, or engage in premarital sex. But if I had to narrow it down to one, that would definitely be premarital sex.

Sexual immorality.

Sexual purity.

The one thing I will never compromise in a dating relationship is my relationship with God.

I would not compromise my principles, or her principles.

Respecting the wishes and spiritual relationship of the other person involved.

I will not make premature committal.

I would not compromise my tastes. For instance, music is important to me. I've seen people go into relationships (usually women) that like one type of music and wind up liking ... let's say country ... just because the other person does.

My spiritual health.

My/her integrity.

Sex, and all that leads up to it. My relationship with God as well, but I did write sex first. If it matters, that stems from my relationship with God.

My faith.

I would not compromise honesty.

Having to deal with stupidity, on any level.

I will not compromise my morals or beliefs. I can compromise on most anything small, but when it comes to my faith or morals, I will not give in.

No way, no how, no whatever will I compromise my faith or the person I'm interested in's faith, or lack thereof.

My relationship with God.

My walk with the Lord.

Whether or not she is a believer.

My faith because that is the cornerstone of my life and I will not let that get in the way.

Not sure I understand the question. I won't marry a non-believer. In the past I wouldn't even date an unbeliever, but I think I am changing my mind on that.

I won't compromise my faith and beliefs. I won't compromise my physical boundaries.

I won't try to change who I am to make a relationship work. If it was meant to be, then you don't have to change

She must be Christian.

Purity of heart, mind, and soul ... of course, it doesn't matter now, because I hope to never date again.

[RELEVANTBOOKS]

FOR MORE INFORMATION ABOUT OTHER RELEVANT BOOKS,

check out www.relevantbooks.com.